JOHN

The Passion of the Son
John 11–21

Group Directory

**Pass this Directory around and have your Group Members
fill in their names and phone numbers**

Name   **Phone**

JOHN
The Passion of the Son

PROJECT DIRECTOR:
James F. Couch, Jr.

WRITING & EDITORIAL TEAM:
Keith Madsen, Cathy Tardif, Katy Harris

PRODUCTION TEAM:
Sharon Penington, Erika Tiepel

SERENDIPITY HOUSE • NASHVILLE, TENNESSEE

© 2002 Serendipity House
All rights reserved
Printed in the United States of America

Published by Serendipity House Publisher
Nashville, Tennessee

International Standard Book Number: 1-57494-096-1

ACKNOWLEDGMENTS

To Zondervan Bible Publishers
for permission to use
the NIV text,
The Holy Bible, New International Bible Society.
© 1973, 1978, 1984 by International Bible Society.
Used by permission of Zondervan Bible Publishers.

Serendipity House
Nashville, Tennessee
1-800-525-9563 / www.serendipityhouse.com

TABLE OF CONTENTS

Session	Reference	Subject	Page
1	John 11:17–44	Lazarus Raised	11
2	John 12:1–16	Jesus at Bethany	19
3	John 13:1–17	Jesus Washes His Disciples' Feet	25
4	John 14:1–21	Jesus Comforts His Disciples	31
5	John 15:1–17	The Vine and the Branches	37
6	John 17:6–23	A Parting Prayer	43
7	John 18:1–11	Jesus is Arrested	49
8	John 18:15–27	Peter's Denials	55
9	John 18:28–40	Jesus Faces Pilate	61
10	John 19:16–37	The Crucifixion	67
11	John 20:1–18	The Empty Tomb	75
12	John 20:19–31	Doubting Thomas	81
13	John 21:1–19	Jesus Reinstates Peter	89

Core Values

Community: The purpose of this curriculum is to build community within the body of believers around Jesus Christ.

Group Process: To build community, the curriculum must be designed to take a group through a step-by-step process of sharing your story with one another.

Interactive Bible Study: To share your "story," the approach to Scripture in the curriculum needs to be open-ended and right brain—to "level the playing field" and encourage everyone to share.

Developmental Stages: To provide a healthy program throughout the four stages of the life cycle of a group, the curriculum needs to offer courses on three levels of commitment: (1) Beginner Level—low-level entry, high structure, to level the playing field; (2) Growth Level—deeper Bible study, flexible structure, to encourage group accountability; (3) Discipleship Level—in-depth Bible study, open structure, to move the group into high gear.

Target Audiences: To build community throughout the culture of the church, the curriculum needs to be flexible, adaptable and transferable into the structure of the average church.

INTRODUCTION

Each healthy small group will move through various stages as it matures.

Growth Stage: Here the group begins to care for one another as it learns to apply what they learn through Bible study, worship and prayer.

Develop Stage: The inductive Bible study deepens while the group members discover and develop gifts and skills. The group explores ways to invite their neighbors and coworkers to group meetings.

Birth Stage: This is the time in which group members form relationships and begin to develop community. The group will spend more time in ice-breaker exercises, relational Bible study and covenant building.

Multiply Stage: The group begins the multiplication process. Members pray about their involvement in new groups. The "new" groups begin the lifecycle again with the Birth Stage.

Subgrouping: If you have nine or more people at a meeting, Serendipity recommends you divide into subgroups of 3–6 for the Bible study. Ask one person to be the leader of each subgroup and to follow the directions for the Bible study. After 30 minutes, the Group Leader will call "time" and ask all subgroups to come together for the Caring Time.

Each group meeting should include all parts of the "three-part agenda."

Ice-Breaker: Fun, history-giving questions are designed to warm the group and to build understanding about the other group members. You can choose to use all of the Ice-Breaker questions, especially if there is a new group member that will need help in feeling comfortable with the group.

Bible Study: The heart of each meeting is the reading and examination of the Bible. The questions are open, discover questions that lead to further inquiry. Reference notes are provided to give everyone a "level playing field." The emphasis is on understanding what the Bible says and applying the truth to real life. The questions for each session build. There is always at least one "going deeper" question provided. You should always leave time for the last of the "questions for interaction." Should you choose, you can use the optional "going deeper" question to satisfy the desire for the challenging questions in groups that have been together for a while.

Caring Time: All study should point us to actions. Each session ends with prayer and direction in caring for the needs of the group members. You can choose between several questions. You should always pray for the "empty chair." Who do you know that could fill that void in your group?

Sharing Your Story: These sessions are designed for members to share a little of their personal lives each time. Through a number of special techniques each member is encouraged to move from low risk less personal sharing to higher risk responses. This helps develop the sense of community and facilitates care giving.

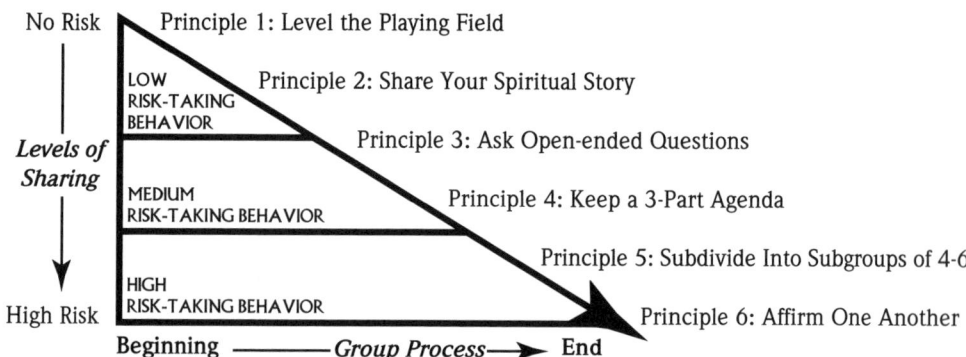

Group Covenant: A group covenant is a "contract" that spells out your expectations and the ground rules for your group. It's very important that your group discuss these issues—preferably as part of the first session.

GROUND RULES:

- *Priority:* While you are in the group, you give the group meeting priority.

- *Participation:* Everyone participates and no one dominates.

- *Respect:* Everyone is given the right to their own opinion and all questions are encouraged and respected.

- *Confidentiality:* Anything that is said in the meeting is never repeated outside the meeting.

- *Empty Chair:* The group stays open to new people at every meeting.

- *Support:* Permission is given to call upon each other in time of need—even in the middle of the night.

- *Advice Giving:* Unsolicited advice is not allowed.

- *Mission:* We agree to do everything in our power to start a new group as our mission.

ISSUES:

- The time and place this group is going to meet is:_____

- Responsibility for refreshments is: _____

- Childcare is _____ responsibility.

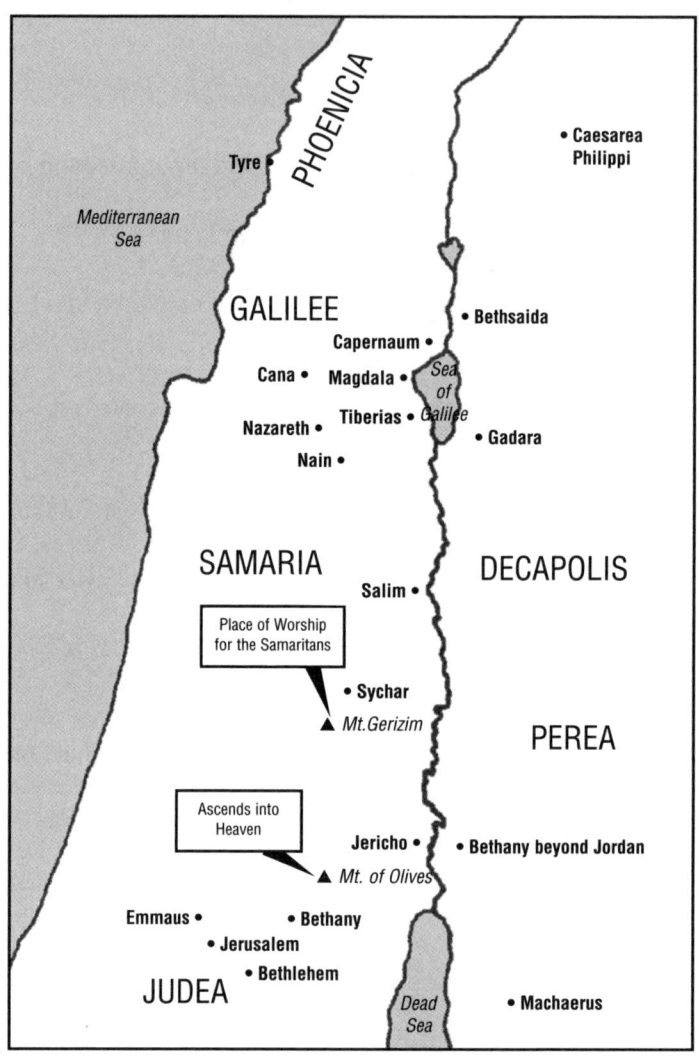

JESUS IN JUDEA

- **Sychar**—Talks with woman at well
- **Emmaus**—Appears to two after resurrection
- **Jericho**—Heals blind Bartimaeus; calls Zacchaeus down from tree
- **Jerusalem**—Clears the temple; crucifixion and resurrection
- **Bethany**—Raises Lazarus from the dead; anointed in Simon the Leper's house
- **Bethlehem**—Birth
- **Bethany beyond Jordan**—Traditional site of the baptism by John the Baptist

SESSION 1
LAZARUS RAISED

SCRIPTURE   JOHN 11:17–44

WELCOME

Welcome to this study of John, chapters 11–21! Together we will learn to appreciate our Savior anew as we follow his passionate earthly ministry to his suffering, death and glorious resurrection. In this second part of the book, the focus shifts to the disciples and Jesus' *private* ministry among them. The theme in this section is the *glory* that is revealed in Jesus' crucifixion and resurrection. The time period of this part is short: from the Thursday night of the Last Supper through Jesus' post-resurrection appearances. We will be dealing with this period later in this study, but we will start a little earlier, with the story of the raising of Lazarus, an event that pointed ahead to Jesus' own death and resurrection.

ICE-BREAKER   15 Min.
CONNECT WITH YOUR GROUP

LEADER

Be sure to read the introductory material in the front of this book prior to this first session. To help your group members get acquainted, have each person introduce him or herself and then take turns answering one or two of the Ice-Breaker questions. If time allows, you may want to discuss all three questions.

Today we are beginning a journey together by studying about one of the most beautiful and powerful miracles of Jesus—that of the raising of Lazarus from the dead. Take some time to get to know one another by sharing your responses to the following questions.

1. Where do you consider your hometown to be? Is it where you were born, where you were raised, or just where you have spent significant years in your life?

2. What death most affected you when you were a child or adolescent? Was it the death of a family member, friend or pet? How did you react at the time?

3. When you cry, what are you most likely to cry about?
   ❏ A sad movie.
   ❏ A sad memory.
   ❏ A beautiful gesture by a loved one.
   ❏ Other_____.

BIBLE STUDY 30 Min.
Read Scripture and Discuss

LEADER
Select a member of the group ahead of time to read aloud the Scripture passage. Then discuss the Questions for Interaction, dividing into subgroups of four or five. Be sure to save time at the end for the Caring Time.

Jesus' own resurrection is not the only one spoken of in Scripture or even the New Testament. Here Jesus raises Lazarus from the dead, in a kind of foreshadowing of his own resurrection. Lazarus was the brother of Mary and Martha, two of Jesus' most faithful followers. Previous to this story, word had been sent to Jesus that Lazarus was ill, but Jesus delayed in returning and in the interim Lazarus died. Read John 11:17–44 and note how Jesus relates to those who are mourning.

Jesus Comforts the Sisters and Raises Lazarus

[17]On his arrival, Jesus found that Lazarus had already been in the tomb for four days. [18]Bethany was less than two miles from Jerusalem, [19]and many Jews had come to Martha and Mary to comfort them in the loss of their brother. [20]When Martha heard that Jesus was coming, she went out to meet him, but Mary stayed at home.

[21]"Lord," Martha said to Jesus, "If you had been here, my brother would not have died. [22]But I know that even now God will give you whatever you ask."

[23]Jesus said to her, "Your brother will rise again."

[24]Martha answered, "I know he will rise again in the resurrection at the last day."

[25]Jesus said to her, "I am the resurrection and the life. He who believes in me will live, even though he dies; [26]and whoever lives and believes in me will never die. Do you believe this?"

[27]"Yes, Lord," she told him, "I believe that you are the Christ, the Son of God, who was to come into the world."

[28]And after she had said this, she went back and called her sister Mary aside. "The Teacher is here," she said, "and is asking for you." [29]When Mary heard this, she got up quickly and went to him. [30]Now Jesus had not yet entered the village, but was still at the place where Martha had met him. [31]When the Jews who had been

with Mary in the house, comforting her, noticed how quickly she got up and went out, they followed her, supposing she was going to the tomb to mourn there.

^{32}When Mary reached the place where Jesus was and saw him, she fell at his feet and said, "Lord, if you had been here, my brother would not have died."

^{33}When Jesus saw her weeping, and the Jews who had come along with her also weeping, he was deeply moved in spirit and troubled. ^{34}"Where have you laid him?" he asked.

"Come and see, Lord," they replied.

^{35}Jesus wept.

^{36}Then the Jews said, "See how he loved him!"

^{37}But some of them said, "Could not he who opened the eyes of the blind man have kept this man from dying?"

^{38}Jesus, once more deeply moved, came to the tomb. It was a cave with a stone laid across the entrance. ^{39}"Take away the stone," he said.

"But, Lord," said Martha, the sister of the dead man, "by this time there is a bad odor, for he has been there four days."

^{40}Then Jesus said, "Did I not tell you that if you believed, you would see the glory of God?"

^{41}So they took away the stone. Then Jesus looked up and said, "Father, I thank you that you have heard me. ^{42}I knew that you always hear me, but I said this for the benefit of the people standing here, that they may believe that you sent me."

^{43}When he had said this, Jesus called in a loud voice, "Lazarus, come out!" ^{44}The dead man came out, his hands and feet wrapped with strips of linen, and a cloth around his face.

Jesus said to them, "Take off the grave clothes and let him go."

John 11:17–44

QUESTIONS FOR INTERACTION

LEADER
Refer to the Summary and Study Notes at the end of this session as needed. If 30 minutes is not enough time to answer all of the questions in this section, conclude the Bible Study by answering questions #6 and #7.

1. When you are sad or hurt, are you more like Martha (immediately reaching out to others for love and support) or Mary (withdrawing to home and only coming out later to others)?

2. When Martha goes out to see Jesus, why do you think Mary stays home?
  ☐ She's irritated with Jesus for not coming earlier.
  ☐ She just wants to be alone for a while.
  ☐ She's tired.
  ☐ Other_____.

3. What do you think Martha was feeling when she said, "If you had been here, my brother would not have died" (v. 21)? What do you think Mary was feeling when she later said the same thing (v. 32)? Were they thinking and feeling the same thing?

4. If Jesus knew he was going to raise Lazarus from the dead, why did he weep? How did those around react to his tears? What does it say to you that Jesus wept?

5. What was the purpose of the prayer that Jesus said just before calling Lazarus forth from the tomb?

6. Where are you right now in terms of this story?
☐ Hiding away at home, instead of going to see Jesus.
☐ Bitter at what might have been had Jesus been around.
☐ Spiritually dead and in the tomb.
☐ Alive, but bound by "grave clothes."
☐ Alive, and free of "grave clothes."

7. What promise of God do you need to believe more fully in order to "see the glory of God"?

GOING DEEPER: *If your group has time and/or wants a challenge, go on to this question.*

8. Both sisters made the statement that if Jesus was with them Lazarus would not have died. Is it always true that if Jesus is truly with us, bad things won't happen? What can we expect of Jesus when he is truly with us?

CARING TIME 15 Min.
APPLY THE LESSON AND PRAY FOR ONE ANOTHER

This very important time is for developing and expressing your concern for each other as group members by praying for one another.

LEADER
Take some extra time in this first session to go over the introductory material at the beginning of this book. At the close, pass around your books and have everyone sign the Group Directory in the front of this book.

1. Agree on the group covenant and ground rules (see the front of this book).

2. What mighty act of God have you seen in your life that you would like the group to join you in thanking God for?

3. Share any other prayer requests and praises, and then close in prayer. Pray specifically for God to lead you to someone to bring next week to fill the empty chair.

NEXT WEEK

Today we explored the incredible miracle of Jesus raising his good friend, Lazarus, from the dead. We saw how moved Jesus is by the grief and suffering of others, and we were reminded of how he weeps with us when we weep and comforts us in our sorrow. In the coming week, take some time to encourage someone who is going through a hard time. Next week we will continue to follow Jesus on his journey to Calvary as he is anointed at Bethany and then triumphantly enters Jerusalem.

NOTES ON JOHN 11:17–44

Summary: The greatest test of any religious faith is what it says to us when we face the reality of death. And so it is that when death comes to the family of some of Jesus' dearest disciples, their faith is challenged. Lazarus, brother of Mary and Martha, becomes seriously ill and the sisters send for Jesus. He delays in coming, however, and Lazarus dies. What will this mean for the faith of Mary and Martha? Will they turn from him in anger and resentment? Although their faith seems to be strained at first, Jesus' gentle affirmation of his power over death reassures them, and when he performs the incredible act of raising Lazarus from the grave, they begin to see the full implication of who Jesus is. The resurrection of Lazarus prepares them for the even more significant resurrection to come—Jesus' own resurrection, a resurrection that paves the way for all who have faith in him to have victory over death itself. Thus, out of what seems to be a great tragedy, a greater victory comes.

11:17 *for four days.* According to a rabbinical tradition, the soul hovers by the grave for three days in the hope of reunion with the body, but at the first sign of decomposition it leaves. Thus by the fourth day, all hope for the person returning to life would be gone.

11:18 *less than two miles from Jerusalem.* This proximity meant that the story of Lazarus being raised to life reached the authorities in Jerusalem quickly. Jesus seemed to use Bethany as a base of operation while he was in Jerusalem (Matt. 21:17).

11:21 *if you had been here, my brother would not have died.* Since Lazarus had died probably even before Jesus received the message (11:1–7), and since Martha also adds a statement of trust in Christ's power to do something wonderful "even now" (v. 22), this is not a rebuke but an expression of regret. It implies faith that if Jesus had been on the scene before his death, Lazarus could have been saved.

11:22 *But I know.* Given Martha's confusion in verse 39, this may not be an expectation of the miracle that does in fact occur. But it is at least an expression of a faith that Christ is in control, and will bring about what is best even now.

11:23 *will rise again.* The Pharisees and other Jewish groups believed in a general resurrection. Martha would have understood Jesus' comment as simply an appropriate expression of comfort at a funeral. Other mourners, wishing to comfort her and assure her that they knew Lazarus had been a good man, probably said very similar things to her.

11:25 *I am the resurrection and the life.* This claim would jar anyone at a funeral! By it, Jesus focuses Martha's attention, not on the doctrine of the general resurrection, but on him as the source of that resurrection (5:24–29). ***will live, even though he dies.*** Spiritual life that will not end by physical death is in view here. In this verse and in verse 26, Jesus is asserting his sovereign power over death and his ability to "give life to whom he is pleased to give it" (5:21).

11:26 *Do you believe this?* Jesus directly confronts Martha with his claim. Does she see him only as a healer or as the Lord of life? Jesus on several occasions made a point of giving his followers an opportunity to declare where they stood in relationship to him. A similar instance is when he asked Peter, "But what about you? ... Who do you say that I am?" (Matt. 16:15).

11:27 In this verse, Martha declares by means of four terms exactly who Jesus is. *Lord.* This can mean simply "sir," a polite form of address. Whereas in verse 21 it may have that intent, in this verse the author is using it in its sense as a title for deity since the rest of Martha's statement is full of spiritual insight into his identity. *Christ, the Son of God, who was to come into the world.* In calling him the Christ, Martha acknowledges Jesus as the One who delivers and saves his people from the power of sin and death. Her recognition of him as the Son of God shows her insight into his divine identity. The meaning behind this title is that he is God, sharing the Father's essential nature just as a child shares the characteristics of his or her parents. It was this claim to be the Son of God that was the real grounds for the opposition against him (19:7). The final phrase, *who was to come into the world*, refers to the expectation that one day a leader like Moses would arise (Deut. 18:18). This too acknowledges his authority and divine commission.

11:32 *Mary.* That Mary stayed at home when Jesus came (v. 20) seems to have been an indication of despair or anger, for otherwise the one who had shown so much devotion to Christ in other situations (Luke 10:38–42; John 11:2) would certainly have come to him right away for comfort. Also, Mary here does not add a statement of faith like Martha expressed, that Jesus still could do something powerful (v. 22). This seems to indicate that when Mary says, "Lord, if you had been here, my brother would not have died," it may have been more an expression of disappointment or anger than faith.

11:33 *weeping.* In contrast to the Western custom of acting in a restrained manner at funerals, in this culture they were times for loud, public expressions of grief. The word "weeping" here indicates this type of wailing.

11:38 *the tomb.* Tombs for people of importance were either vertical shafts covered by a stone, or horizontal hollows carved out of a hill. Since this tomb is carved out of a cave, it would be the latter type.

11:40 *Did I not tell you.* This may be a reference to the message in verse 4, or the implication of what he meant by his declaration to Martha in verse 25. The signs in this Gospel have consistently been regarded as demonstrations of Jesus' identity. They reveal his glory (2:11) and, based on them, people make decisions about who he is (6:14; 9:32–33). This final sign will reveal what has been alluded to all along—Jesus is God.

11:44 *wrapped with strips of linen.* While burial customs included wrapping the body with cloth and spices (John 19:40), this was not intended to preserve the body, like the ancient Egyptian process of mummification, but only as a sign of honor for the deceased person.

SESSION 2
JESUS ANOINTED AT BETHANY

SCRIPTURE   JOHN 12:1–16

LAST WEEK

In last week's session we considered the incredible miracle of Jesus raising Lazarus from the dead, and how this was a precursor to his own resurrection. We were also reminded of how Jesus understands our sorrows and weeps with us when we go through grief and loss. This week we follow Jesus as he heads toward the events that lead up to his death and resurrection, specifically his anointing at Bethany and the Triumphal Entry.

ICE-BREAKER  15 Min.
CONNECT WITH YOUR GROUP

LEADER
Begin the session with a word of prayer. Have your group members take turns sharing their responses to one, two or all three of the Ice-Breaker questions. Be sure that everyone gets a chance to participate.

Today we will see how those who loved Jesus honored him and showed their appreciation for all he had done. Take turns sharing some of your unique experiences celebrating with family and friends.

1. What town, other than your own, do you remember going to as a child or adolescent to visit family or friends? What did you look forward to doing while you were there? Who did you look forward to seeing?

2. When you were an adolescent, what was the most memorable event you can remember being held to honor you or an accomplishment you achieved?
   ❏ A special birthday party.
   ❏ A graduation party.
   ❏ Other_____.

   How did you feel about the experience?

3. What is most often your style of entering a party?
- ❒ Stylishly late, with lots of fanfare.
- ❒ Quietly slipping in.
- ❒ Coming early to see how I can help.
- ❒ Other_____.

BIBLE STUDY — 30 Min.
Read Scripture and Discuss

LEADER

Select three members of the group ahead of time to read aloud the Scripture passage. Have one member read John's narration; one member read for Judas; and one member read for Jesus. Have the whole group read together the part of the crowd. Then divide into subgroups of four or five and discuss the Questions for Interaction.

Virtually everything that happens in this section of John points toward Jesus' death and resurrection. He is anointed with perfume at Bethany, and he interprets this act as preparation for his death. He enters Jerusalem, the city in which he is about to die, with great fanfare in recognition of his special kingship and the saving act he is about to perform. It is like a bullfighter entering the ring. Read John 12:1–16 and note how Jesus responds to these acts of love and appreciation.

Jesus Anointed at Bethany and the Triumphal Entry

John: **12** *Six days before the Passover, Jesus arrived at Bethany, where Lazarus lived, whom Jesus had raised from the dead. ²Here a dinner was given in Jesus' honor. Martha served, while Lazarus was among those reclining at the table with him. ³Then Mary took about a pint of pure nard, an expensive perfume; she poured it on Jesus' feet and wiped his feet with her hair. And the house was filled with the fragrance of the perfume. ⁴But one of his disciples, Judas Iscariot, who was later to betray him, objected,*

Judas: *⁵"Why wasn't this perfume sold and the money given to the poor? It was worth a year's wages."*

John: *⁶He did not say this because he cared about the poor but because he was a thief; as keeper of the money bag, he used to help himself to what was put into it.*

Jesus: *⁷"Leave her alone," Jesus replied. "It was intended that she should save this perfume for the day of my burial. ⁸You will always have the poor among you, but you will not always have me."*

John: *⁹Meanwhile a large crowd of Jews found out that Jesus was there and came, not only because of him but also to see Lazarus, whom he had raised from*

	the dead. ¹⁰So the chief priests made plans to kill Lazarus as well, ¹¹for on account of him many of the Jews were going over to Jesus and putting their faith in him. ¹²The next day the great crowd that had come for the Feast heard that Jesus was on his way to Jerusalem. ¹³They took palm branches and went out to meet him, shouting,
Crowd:	*"Hosanna! Blessed is he who comes in the name of the Lord! Blessed is the King of Israel!"*
John:	*¹⁴Jesus found a young donkey and sat upon it, as it is written, ¹⁵"Do not be afraid, O Daughter of Zion; see, your king is coming, seated on a donkey's colt." ¹⁶At first his disciples did not understand all this. Only after Jesus was glorified did they realize that these things had been written about him and that they had done these things to him.*

John 12:1–16

QUESTIONS FOR INTERACTION

LEADER
Refer to the Summary and Study Notes at the end of this session as needed. If 30 minutes is not enough time to answer all of the questions in this section, conclude the Bible Study by answering questions #6 and #7.

1. Who are you most like in the story of the anointing at Bethany?
   - ❐ Mary—extravagant, but moved by my feelings.
   - ❐ Martha—always ready to serve.
   - ❐ Lazarus—just happy to be alive.
   - ❐ Judas—penny-pinching and practical.

2. What motivated Mary to anoint Jesus' feet with this expensive perfume?
   - ❐ An understanding that his death was coming.
   - ❐ Affection.
   - ❐ Respect.
   - ❐ Other_____.

3. How does Jesus seem to feel about Mary's act? How would you have felt had you been in his place?

4. What does Jesus mean to imply when he says, "You will always have the poor among you, but you will not always have me" (v. 8)?

5. What do you think the crowds were expecting when they welcomed Jesus to Jerusalem with such fanfare? Were their expectations in line with what God had planned for Jesus?

6. In relation to your own spiritual journey, where are you right now, in terms of these stories?
   - ❒ Like the chief priests and Pharisees—fighting any evidence of the supernatural.
   - ❒ Like the crowd—just wanting to praise Jesus.
   - ❒ Like Mary—looking for ways to express my love.
   - ❒ Other_____.

7. If you had more of the spirit of Mary, what act of loving service would you be doing for Jesus right now?

GOING DEEPER: *If your group has time and/or wants a challenge, go on to this question.*

8. When you (or your church) has to decide between investing money in the needs of the poor or people in need, and investing money in a symbol of religious devotion (like a building or work of artistic expression), how do you decide which should have highest priority? How does your answer relate to what Jesus says in verse 8?

CARING TIME   15 Min.
APPLY THE LESSON AND PRAY FOR ONE ANOTHER

LEADER
Bring the group members back together and begin the Caring Time by sharing responses to all three questions. Then share prayer requests and praises. Be sure to take turns so everyone gets a chance to participate.

Jesus' disciples made a special effort in today's passage to show him they cared. Care for one another now by encouraging and supporting one another in a time of sharing and prayer.

1. What special act of caring, like Mary's anointing of Jesus, has been done for you recently? How would you like to thank God for this act?

2. What are you, like the disciples (v. 16), not understanding? How can this group be in prayer for you, that you might understand more?

3. What can you do in the coming week to show Jesus how much you appreciate him?

P.S. *Add new group members to the Group Directory in the front of this book.*

> **NEXT WEEK**
>
> Today we looked at Jesus' anointing at Bethany and his triumphal entry into Jerusalem. We were reminded of Jesus' love for us, and how we need to love him and appreciate him in return. In the coming week, be sure to follow through on your response to question #3 in the Caring Time. Next week we will see what we can discover about the beautiful and humble act of Jesus washing his disciples' feet during the Last Supper.

NOTES ON JOHN 12:1–16

Summary: This section of John presents an interesting comparison between two acts honoring Jesus Christ and who he was: his anointing with perfume by Mary at Bethany, and the spreading of palm branches in his path by the crowd in Jerusalem. Mary's anointing of him was a servant act, like the washing of feet, but taken to a different level. She poured expensive perfume on his feet and then wiped them with her hair. What an act of humility! Was it done with an awareness of his coming death? We really don't know. But we do know that the devotion shown was one with real depth. It was born of gratitude for what Jesus had done in raising her brother, and it was part of a discipleship that continued through Christ's death to his resurrection.

The action of the crowd was also a servant act. The spreading of the palm branches, in order to soften the path of Christ's ride, was an honor one would do for a king. Indeed they proclaimed, "Blessed is the King of Israel!" However, there was a false expectation attached to this act that changed its significance. Many, if not all, of those who spread palm branches were expecting a king who would be a military leader who would free them from Rome. When this expectation didn't occur, their devotion proved shallow and they turned away from him. This contrast presents us with an important question we need to answer: Is our devotion to Christ full of false, self-serving expectations, like the crowd; or is it full of true gratefulness and honoring of him, in the spirit of Mary?

12:1 *Bethany.* A small town just a couple of miles from Jerusalem. Jesus seemed to use Bethany as a base of operation while he was in Jerusalem (Matt. 21:17).

12:2 *Martha served.* This is quite consistent with the role Martha took on other occasions when Jesus came (Luke 10:38–42). Unlike the story in Luke, Martha does not complain about her role here.

23

12:3 *pure nard*. This was a perfume derived from the spikenard plant and produced in the Himalayas.

12:6 *he was a thief*. This is the only place in the Gospels that we are given any background about Judas. The author's point is not to dismiss legitimate caring for the poor, but to point out that in spite of his words Judas' motives were self-serving.

12:7 *perfume for the day of my burial*. Jesus uses this incident as a foreshadowing of his death. In that culture bodies were often wrapped with spices for burial (19:39–40). Jesus' statement does not mean that Mary was aware of this purpose—it is far more likely that she meant it as an act of thanksgiving to Jesus for what he had done for her brother.

12:8 *You will always have the poor*. This is not meant to disparage acts of mercy, but to shift the focus onto the upcoming death of Jesus. In contrast to the poor, Jesus would not always be around to honor in this way. That this is not meant to discount the need to help the poor can be seen in the fact that Jesus here is referring to Deuteronomy 15:11, where the statement is made, "There will always be poor people in the land." There the statement is followed up with the command, "Therefore I command you to be openhanded toward your brothers and toward the poor and needy in your land."

12:9 *a large crowd of Jews*. "Jews" here does not mean the Jewish authorities, as it often does in John's Gospel, but simply Jewish people in general.

12:10 *the chief priests made plans to kill Lazarus as well*. There is no record that this ironic plot to kill a man who had just been raised from the dead ever got beyond the planning stage.

12:12 *the great crowd*. This was obviously a very large crowd of Jews in town for the Passover. Jerusalem was a city of normally under 25,000 people. When Passover was celebrated the population greatly increased to 4 or 5 times its normal size.

12:13 *palm branches*. The other Gospels mention people using their garments as well. ***Hosanna!*** Originally a one-word prayer for God to save (Ps. 118:25), this had become an expression of praise. ***Blessed is he who comes in the name of the Lord!*** Psalm 118:26 was used in the liturgy for Passover and celebrated God's deliverance of Israel from her enemies.

SESSION 3
JESUS WASHES HIS DISCIPLES' FEET

SCRIPTURE   JOHN 13:1–17

LAST WEEK

Just prior to Jesus' suffering and death, he was honored by two beautiful servant acts—the anointing with perfume by Mary at Bethany and the triumphal entry into Jerusalem. We discussed these events last week and were reminded to continue to find our own ways to honor Jesus and thank him for all he has done for us. This week we will study a servant act by Jesus: the washing of his disciples' feet. In looking at this act, we will consider what it means to serve in Jesus' name.

ICE-BREAKER   15 Min.
CONNECT WITH YOUR GROUP

LEADER
Begin the session with prayer, asking God for his blessing and presence. Choose one or two Ice-Breaker questions. If you have a new group member you may want to do all three. Remember to stick closely to the three-part agenda and the time allowed for each segment.

"Actions speak louder than words" is an old saying that we've often heard through the years. Helping others and doing random acts of kindness can truly touch the lives of loved ones and strangers alike. Take turns sharing your own experiences with being a "servant" to others.

1. When you were a child or adolescent, what "servant" tasks did you have to do in the household?
   ❏ Washing the dishes.
   ❏ Taking out the garbage.
   ❏ Cleaning the bathrooms.
   ❏ Other_____.

   How did you feel about doing these jobs?

2. What "servant" jobs do you find yourself having to do today? Have your feelings about doing these tasks changed since you were a child?

3. In your family today, what acts do you perform to let each other know how much you care for one another? When has such an act been especially important to you?

BIBLE STUDY 30 Min.
Read Scripture and Discuss

LEADER

Have a member of the group, selected ahead of time, read aloud the Scripture passage. Then discuss the Questions for Interaction, dividing into smaller subgroups of four or five.

Jesus modeled a different kind of leadership than the world was used to seeing. As we saw last week, instead of entering Jerusalem on a warhorse, like a king might normally do, he entered on a humble servant animal. In this week's lesson, he continues that kind of modeling. Instead of demanding service of others, he strips to what a servant would wear, and he washes his disciples' feet. This was a servant act of unheard humility for a respected religious teacher. But Jesus wanted his disciples to know that the way to the kingdom of God was not through demanding privilege, but through serving others in love; and to teach them this, he had to model it. Read John 13:1–17 and note how the disciples react to Jesus.

Jesus Washes His Disciples' Feet

13 *It was just before the Passover Feast. Jesus knew that the time had come for him to leave this world and go to the Father. Having loved his own who were in the world, he now showed them the full extent of his love.*

²The evening meal was being served, and the devil had already prompted Judas Iscariot, son of Simon, to betray Jesus. ³Jesus knew that the Father had put all things under his power, and that he had come from God and was returning to God; ⁴so he got up from the meal, took off his outer clothing, and wrapped a towel around his waist. ⁵After that, he poured water into a basin and began to wash his disciples' feet, drying them with the towel that was wrapped around him.

⁶He came to Simon Peter, who said to him, "Lord, are you going to wash my feet?"

⁷Jesus replied, "You do not realize now what I am doing, but later you will understand."

⁸"No," said Peter, "you shall never wash my feet."

Jesus answered, "Unless I wash you, you have no part with me."

⁹"Then, Lord," Simon Peter replied, "not just my feet but my hands and my head as well!"

¹⁰Jesus answered, "A person who has had a bath needs only to wash his feet; his whole body is clean. And you are clean, though not every one of you." ¹¹For he knew who was going to betray him, and that was why he said not every one was clean.

¹²When he had finished washing their feet, he put on his clothes and returned to his place. "Do you understand what I have done for you?" he asked them. ¹³"You call me 'Teacher' and 'Lord,' and rightly so, for that is what I am. ¹⁴Now that I, your Lord and Teacher, have washed your feet, you also should wash one another's feet. ¹⁵I have set you an example that you should do as I have done for you. ¹⁶I tell you the truth, no servant is greater than his master, nor is a messenger greater than the one who sent him. ¹⁷Now that you know these things, you will be blessed if you do them.

John 13:1–17

LEADER

Refer to the Summary and Study Notes at the end of this session as needed. If 30 minutes is not enough time to answer all of the questions in this section, conclude the Bible Study by answering questions #6 and #7.

QUESTIONS FOR INTERACTION

1. How easy is it for you, like Jesus does here, to show someone "the full extent" of your love (v. 1)?

2. What three things does Jesus know about himself, according to verse 3? What influence does this kind of self-knowledge have on what Jesus is about to do?

3. What was Simon Peter feeling when he balked at Jesus washing his feet? What do you think Jesus meant when he said, "Unless I wash you, you have no part with me" (v. 8)?

4. Why does Jesus say that not every one of the disciples is clean (v. 10)?
   ❏ He is trying to give Judas one last chance to change his mind.
   ❏ He is trying to warn the others.
   ❏ He is just showing his complete knowledge of the situation.
   ❏ Other_____.

5. What does Jesus mean when he calls upon the disciples to "wash one another's feet" (v. 14)? Is he starting a new ritual, or does the statement have a broader significance?

6. Looking back at verse 3, which kind of self-knowledge do you have the hardest time with?
   ❏ Knowing my own power and ability.
   ❏ Knowing my roots, the power of my heritage.
   ❏ Knowing where I am going in life.

   How can this group help you increase your self-knowledge in this area?

7. What is harder for you, to humble yourself enough to serve others or to humble yourself enough to let them serve you? Why?

   GOING DEEPER: *If your group has time and/or wants a challenge, go on to this question.*

8. Does the church today truly have a servant leadership? What can we do to help our leaders become more servant-minded?

CARING TIME   15 Min.
APPLY THE LESSON AND PRAY FOR ONE ANOTHER

LEADER

Begin the Caring Time by having group members take turns sharing responses to all three questions. Be sure to save at least the last five minutes for a time of group prayer. Remember to include a prayer for the empty chair when concluding the prayer time.

Knowing that Jesus wants to show you "the full extent of his love," gather together now and encourage and support one another with a time of sharing and prayer.

1. How is your relationship with Jesus right now?
   ❏ Close.
   ❏ Distant.
   ❏ Improving.
   ❏ Strained.
   ❏ Growing apart.
   ❏ Other_____.

2. Who has mentored you on how to be a servant-leader? Take time to thank God for the example of this person.

3. In what ways can the members of this group "wash one another's feet" and serve each other in love?

> **NEXT WEEK**
>
> Today we were inspired by the wonderful example of serving that Jesus modeled for us when he humbly washed the disciples' feet. We were reminded that he did this so we would then go and "wash one another's feet." In the coming week, follow through on your response to question #3 in the Caring Time, or do a special act of service for a family member or friend. Next week we will listen to Jesus as he comforts his disciples with some reassuring words in anticipation of his having to leave them to go to his Father in heaven.

NOTES ON JOHN 13:1–17

Summary: Most of the second half of John consists of pointing the way toward Christ's death and resurrection. In that context, the story of Jesus washing his disciples' feet is really a story of Jesus preparing the disciples for his departure. They needed to know what kind of leadership was going to be expected of them after he was no longer directly available to teach and lead them on earth.

In other Gospels the issue is raised at this point regarding which of them is the greatest, and the mother of James and John comes along to speak for places of honor for her two sons. But in the washing of the disciples' feet, Jesus is saying that servant leadership is needed, not egotistical, power-hungry leadership. History proved him correct. When the followers of Christ were being persecuted for their faith, and people were losing loved ones to Nero and others, a servant leadership was needed that comforted, consoled and helped those who were hurting to be lifted up. The followers of Christ would experience enough of power-hungry leadership as they confronted the officials of Rome and the jealous religious leadership of non-believing Jews. They would need a more healing alternative, not only for themselves, but also for the world they wished to influence in Christ's name. In the washing of his disciples' feet, Christ was showing them what such leadership would need to look like.

13:1 *Jesus knew.* Here, as well as in verses 3 and 11, John emphasizes what Jesus knew. This lays stress on the fact that Jesus was in charge of the events leading to his death (10:18). ***the full extent of his love.*** Jesus did not only have knowledge; he also had *love.* Knowledge and power without love would have been less than a full revelation of God.

13:3 Jesus' self-knowledge was at the heart of his willingness and ability to serve. This verse says he knew who he was in terms of where he had come from (the Father), where he was going (back to the Father), and what his role was while he was here. It is the people who are unsure of their identity, and thus have something to prove, who have difficulty humbling themselves to serve others.

13:4–5 The lowest-ranking servant in the household normally washed people's dusty, sandaled feet before a meal was served. Jesus' action was deliberate. Removing his outer clothing was a sign he was going to do some work, and it would have identified him with a servant who generally worked in minimal garb. The other Gospels mention that at the Last Supper there was a discussion among the Twelve about who was the greatest (Luke 22:24). In that context, Jesus identified the greatest as the one who was the servant (Luke 22:25–26).

13:6 Lord, are you going to wash my feet? Peter, recognizing the impropriety of a master washing the servants' feet, protests. The Greek sentence actually reads more like, "You? Wash *my* feet?" Peter is appalled at this breach of normal procedure.

13:7 later you will understand. This may simply be referring to verse 17, but more likely it refers to the full understanding of Jesus' servanthood that will be made clear after his resurrection.

13:8 Unless I wash you, you have no part with me. This lifts the meaning of the foot washing to a higher plane than simply that of an object lesson about humility. Jesus' foot washing was a symbol of the spiritual cleansing he would accomplish for his followers through the Cross.

13:10 *A person who has had a bath.* Jesus uses the picture of a person who, after washing completely, travels somewhere. Upon arrival, only his feet need to be washed to be clean again. ***you are clean, though not every one of you.*** Literally, "though not all"—which leaves the meaning ambiguous to the hearers. He may mean only that they are literally still not all clean, but the context shows his real intent was to prepare them for his startling announcement in verse 21.

13:14 *you also should wash one another's feet.* Some Christian groups have taken this literally, making it an ordinance or sacrament, like baptism and communion. However, most would take this to mean that we are called to serve one another in the spirit of Christ.

13:16 *no servant is greater than his master.* If the master serves, how much more should the servants do so? ***a messenger.*** This is the same word as "apostle," which only occurs here in this Gospel. An apostle was a person sent with the authority to represent the one who sent him. Jesus' followers are to represent his servanthood to others.

Session 4
Jesus Comforts His Disciples
Scripture John 14:1–21

LAST WEEK

In last week's session we watched as Jesus modeled for us a beautiful example of humble servanthood by washing his disciples' feet, a task usually performed by the lowliest of servants. We were reminded that Jesus did this so we would also practice servant leadership and "wash one another's feet." This week we will consider some words of comfort Jesus shared with his disciples as he prepared them for his departure and what those encouraging words say to us today.

ICE-BREAKER 15 Min.
Connect With Your Group

LEADER
Choose one, two or all three of the Ice-Breaker questions. Welcome and introduce new group members and begin with a word of prayer.

Jesus knew that life wouldn't be easy for his disciples when he left them. He also knows it's not easy for us today, so his words of comfort in today's passage are meant just as much for us. Take turns sharing your experiences with finding comfort in this world.

1. What was the house or apartment like that you lived in when you were in grade school? How many rooms were in it, and what room gave you the most comfort?

2. In what ways do you look like your father? In what ways are you like him in personality? In what ways are you different from him? How do you feel about being like or different from your father?

31

3. When you got upset or worried as a child, what was your main source of comfort?
- ❏ My mother or father.
- ❏ A sibling.
- ❏ A best friend or pet.
- ❏ Eating a "comfort food" like ice cream.
- ❏ Other_____.

BIBLE STUDY 30 Min.
READ SCRIPTURE AND DISCUSS

LEADER
Have a member of the group, selected ahead of time, read aloud the Scripture passage. Then discuss the Questions for Interaction, dividing into smaller subgroups of four or five. Be sure to save at least 15–20 minutes at the end for the Caring Time.

Great leaders oftentimes have given famous farewell speeches to those they have led. One example of this is General MacArthur's farewell to his troops when he said, "I shall return!" Another example is a speech that Martin Luther King, Jr. gave when he spoke of the "Promised Land" and said, "I may not get there with you." In the following passage, Jesus similarly says farewell to his "troops," and makes some important promises to them about his abiding presence through the Spirit. These promises say much to us as well. Read John 14:1–21 and note these comforting promises.

Jesus Comforts His Disciples

14 *"Do not let your hearts be troubled. Trust in God; trust also in me. ²In my Father's house are many rooms; if it were not so, I would have told you. I am going there to prepare a place for you. ³And if I go and prepare a place for you, I will come back and take you to be with me that you also may be where I am. ⁴You know the way to the place where I am going."*

⁵Thomas said to him, "Lord, we don't know where you are going, so how can we know the way?"

⁶Jesus answered, "I am the way and the truth and the life. No one comes to the Father except through me. ⁷If you really knew me, you would know my Father as well. From now on, you do know him and have seen him."

⁸Philip said, "Lord, show us the Father and that will be enough for us."

⁹Jesus answered: "Don't you know me, Philip, even after I have been among you such a long time? Anyone who has seen me has seen the Father. How can you say, 'Show us the Father'? ¹⁰Don't you believe that I am in the Father, and that the Father is in me? The words I say to you are not just my own. Rather, it is the Father, living in me, who is doing his work. ¹¹*Believe me when I say that I am in the Father and the Father is in me; or at least believe on the evidence of the miracles themselves.* ¹²*I tell you the truth, anyone who has faith in me will do what I have been doing. He will do even greater things than these, because I am going to the Father.* ¹³*And I will do whatever you ask in my name, so that the Son may bring glory to the Father.* ¹⁴*You may ask me for anything in my name, and I will do it.*

¹⁵*"If you love me, you will obey what I command.* ¹⁶*And I will ask the Father, and he will give you another Counselor to be with you forever*—¹⁷*the Spirit of truth. The world cannot accept him, because it neither sees him nor knows him. But you know him, for he lives with you and will be in you.* ¹⁸*I will not leave you as orphans; I will come to you.* ¹⁹*Before long, the world will not see me anymore, but you will see me. Because I live, you also will live.* ²⁰*On that day you will realize that I am in my Father, and you are in me, and I am in you.* ²¹*Whoever has my commands and obeys them, he is the one who loves me. He who loves me will be loved by my Father, and I too will love him and show myself to him."*

John 14:1–21

QUESTIONS FOR INTERACTION

> **LEADER**
>
> Refer to the Summary and Study Notes at the end of the session as needed. If 30 minutes is not enough time to answer all of the questions in this section, conclude the Bible Study by answering questions #6 and #7.

1. What reassurance does Jesus mean to convey when he says, "In my father's house are many rooms" (v. 2)?
   - ❏ There's room for everyone.
   - ❏ There is provision for different kinds of people (in different kinds of rooms).
   - ❏ Other_____.

2. What three things does Jesus say he is in verse 6? What do these three designations say to you about Jesus and his mission?

3. How do we know what the Father is like? What do we learn about the Father through that source?

4. How can Jesus say that the disciples will be able to do "even greater" things than he has been doing (see note on verse 12)? In what ways will they be greater? What empowers a disciple to do such great things?

5. What does Jesus mean when he says he will not leave the disciples "as orphans" (v. 18)?

6. When, if ever, have you felt like an "orphan," like you were all alone in the world with no one to care for you?

7. When you feel like an orphan, or when your heart is troubled (v. 1), how hard is it for you to trust God and his promises? What would make it easier for you to trust God?
   ❐ More support from other Christians.
   ❐ More evidence of God's faithfulness.
   ❐ Other_____.

GOING DEEPER: *If your group has time and/or wants a challenge, go on to this question.*

8. Jesus says in verse 14, "You may ask me for anything in my name, and I will do it." Does this apply to requests for material possessions and wealth, or just to spiritual help? Given this promise, why are so many Christians struggling?

CARING TIME 15 Min.
APPLY THE LESSON AND PRAY FOR ONE ANOTHER

LEADER
Be sure to save at least 15 minutes for this important time. After sharing responses to all three questions and asking for prayer requests, close in a time of group prayer.

Once again, take some time now to comfort each other with God's love by sharing your responses to the following questions and praying for one another.

1. When has Christ come to you at a time when you were feeling like an orphan? Thank him for his comfort and presence during that difficult time.

2. In the spirit of verse 14, what would you like to ask Jesus for right now?

3. Pray for the person on your right, that God would send the Counselor, the Holy Spirit, to be with him or her in a special way during the week to come.

NEXT WEEK

Today we looked at some words of comfort that Jesus said to his disciples in anticipation of his having to leave them to go to his Father in heaven. We were reminded of the many beautiful promises that Jesus gave us, promises that give us hope and perseverance. In the coming week, memorize one or two of the promises in today's Scripture that were especially meaningful to you. Next week we will consider the descriptive teaching of Jesus that compares himself to a vine and his followers to the dependent branches. He will also remind us once again of his ultimate command: Love each other.

NOTES on JOHN 14:1–21

Summary: A natural question to ask when Jesus' earthly ministry was almost through would have been, "What happens next?" This chapter is the answer to that question. Actually, this chapter tells both what was next for Jesus and what was next for the disciples and the world. Jesus' next step was to go to the Father to prepare a place for believers (vv. 2–3). This was an important reassurance to the disciples who had learned to love him. He wouldn't just cease to exist, and he wouldn't go somewhere where they would never see him again. The disciples' next step was to receive the Holy Spirit. This would do essentially two things for them: (1) it would bring them comfort and direction (vv. 16–18), and (2) it would enable them to do "even greater" works than Jesus himself had done (v. 12). This was also an important reassurance to the disciples, because it told them that what Jesus had started would not be left entirely on their shoulders, nor would it be allowed to simply languish. They were part of a kingdom that would not fail, and that is indeed good news for them and us.

14:1 *Do not let your hearts be troubled.* Having settled his own mind and heart, Jesus brings comfort to the disciples by giving them hope. These words of comfort were probably given because they had been made anxious by Jesus' words in 13:33.

14:2 *my Father's house.* In John 2:16 this referred to the temple. Here, it means heaven. The earthly temple was seen to be a symbol of the actual dwelling place of God (Heb. 9:24). ***many rooms.*** Literally, "dwelling places." The emphasis is not on having separate compartments in heaven, but on the abundance of room for all who will receive Jesus.

14:3 *I will come back.* This probably refers to the coming of Christ through his Spirit (vv. 15–21) rather than to the Second Coming, which receives very little attention in this Gospel. Through the Spirit, Jesus "returns" to the disciples (v. 18), and they are then "in" or "with" him and the Father (vv. 20,23). Seen in this way, this promise is not for the distant future, but will be true for the disciples in a very short time (20:22).

14:6 *I am the way.* The destination to which Jesus is going is not so much a place, but a person—the Father (7:33; 8:21). The way for the disciples to come to the Father is through the Son, who, by his death, opens the way for them (Heb. 10:19–22).

14:7 *you would know my Father as well.* John has previously written, "No one has ever seen God, but God the One and Only, who is at the Father's side, has made him known" (1:18). Paul wrote of Jesus in Colossians 1:15, "He is the image of the invisible God." All of this says that to know what Jesus is like is to know what God the Father is like.

14:11 *believe on the evidence of the miracles.* The "signs" in chapters 1–12 were all given to point to the truth that Jesus came to reveal God's glory and bring life to people.

14:12 *He will do even greater things.* The work Jesus has done is not so much tied up with miracles as it is with revealing the truth about God. It is this mission that his disciples will inherit. The "greater" things that they will do should be understood in terms of their scope (i.e., it is the disciples who will bring the Gospel to the Gentile world) rather than their power.

14:14 *You may ask me for anything.* See Matthew 7:7–11. It is assumed these requests will be done from the perspective of the faith of one who is seeking first the kingdom (Matt. 6:33). When we seek first the kingdom, God answers our requests for our needs.

14:16 *another Counselor.* The Greek term *paraclete* is a rich term for which there is no sufficient English translation. Attempts such as "Counselor" or "Helper" or "Comforter" fail because they emphasize only one of many aspects of the term. Since this discourse presents the ministry of the Spirit in the same terms as that of Jesus, the Spirit can be referred to as *another* "Paraclete" like Jesus (1 John 2:1).

14:17 *The world cannot accept him.* Just as the "world" has not accepted Jesus or the Father (5:37–38), neither will it be able to receive the Spirit. ***he lives with you and will be in you.*** This parallelism does not create distinctions between "with" and "in," but simply adds emphasis to Jesus' dramatic announcement. The reality of the indwelling Spirit lifts the Old Testament expectation of a new covenant, wherein God would dwell with his people, to unimaginable heights (Isa. 7:14; Jer. 31:31–34; Ezek. 34:30). It is this indwelling of the Spirit with God's people that ultimately makes the temple and the issue of where to worship irrelevant (4:21).

14:18 *I will not leave you as orphans.* When a rabbi died, his disciples were spoken of as being orphaned. ***I will come to you.*** In this context, the coming of Jesus spoken of here should be understood in terms of the coming of the Spirit. It is in that way that they will "see" him, whereas the world will not (v. 19).

14:20 *On that day.* This speaks of the time when the Spirit will be given to the disciples.

Session 5
The Vine and the Branches
Scripture John 15:1–17

LAST WEEK

Jesus knew it would be difficult for his disciples when he was no longer physically with them, so in last week's Scripture passage we listened in as he offered comforting words to his followers, both present and future. We were also reminded of many wonderful promises given by Jesus that help us to persevere on our daily spiritual journey. This week we will look at the intimate connection we have with Jesus, which he described as being like the relationship between a vine and its branches.

ICE-BREAKER   15 Min.
Connect With Your Group

LEADER
Begin the session with a word of prayer, asking God for his blessing and presence. To help new group members get acquainted, remember to do all three Ice-Breaker questions.

Jesus often used earthly examples to explain heavenly concepts. Today we will learn how much he loves us and is connected to us through the concept of the vine and its branches. Take turns responding to the following questions and share some of your unique life experiences in metaphorical terms.

1. When you consider your "family tree," what kind of tree is it most like?
   ❏ A mighty oak with strong, symmetrical branches.
   ❏ A scraggly mountain pine.
   ❏ A fruit tree that feeds the neighborhood.
   ❏ Any kind of tree that has a lot of nuts.
   ❏ Other_____.

37

2. If you were to compare what you have accomplished in the past year to a crop, what kind of crop would it be?
- ❏ A bumper crop.
- ❏ Above-average yield.
- ❏ Enough to survive off of.
- ❏ Pretty drought-stricken.
- ❏ Other_____.

3. What do you consider the greatest act of friendship that has been done for you? Describe how this act affected you using weather terms.

BIBLE STUDY   30 Min.
READ SCRIPTURE AND DISCUSS

LEADER
Have a member of the group, selected ahead of time, read aloud the Scripture passage. Then discuss the Questions for Interaction, dividing into smaller subgroups of four or five.

The American ideal is sometimes seen as the John Wayne-type hero who stands alone. However, Jesus taught the importance of relationship and interdependence. In the following passage, he emphasizes to his disciples that they can't be "Lone Rangers," but they're to be like branches that have to stay attached to the vine in order to bear fruit. In our day and age, with so many challenges before us, we also need to maintain this intimate connection with our Lord and Savior. Read John 15:1–17 and note what it means to truly love God and one another.

The Vine and the Branches

15 *"I am the true vine, and my Father is the gardener. ²He cuts off every branch in me that bears no fruit, while every branch that does bear fruit he prunes so that it will be even more fruitful. ³You are already clean because of the word I have spoken to you. ⁴Remain in me, and I will remain in you. No branch can bear fruit by itself; it must remain in the vine. Neither can you bear fruit unless you remain in me.*

⁵"I am the vine; you are the branches. If a man remains in me and I in him, he will bear much fruit; apart from me you can do nothing. ⁶If anyone does not remain in me, he is like a branch that is thrown away and withers; such branches are picked up, thrown into the fire and burned. ⁷If you remain in me and my words remain in you, ask whatever you wish, and it will be given you. ⁸This is to my Father's glory, that you bear much fruit, showing yourselves to be my disciples.

⁹*"As the Father has loved me, so have I loved you. Now remain in my love. ¹⁰If you obey my commands, you will remain in my love, just as I have obeyed my Father's commands and remain in his love. ¹¹I have told you this so that my joy may be in you and that your joy may be complete. ¹²My command is this: Love each other as I have loved you. ¹³Greater love has no one than this, that he lay down his life for his friends. ¹⁴You are my friends if you do what I command. ¹⁵I no longer call you servants, because a servant does not know his master's business. Instead, I have called you friends, for everything that I learned from my Father I have made known to you. ¹⁶You did not choose me, but I chose you and appointed you to go and bear fruit—fruit that will last. Then the Father will give you whatever you ask in my name. ¹⁷This is my command: Love each other.*

John 15:1–17

LEADER

Refer to the Summary and Study Notes at the end of this session as needed. If 30 minutes is not enough time to answer all of the questions in this section, conclude the Bible Study by answering question #7.

QUESTIONS FOR INTERACTION

1. Had you been one of the disciples when Jesus first said these things, how would you have reacted?
   - ❏ "Zip! Right over my head!"
   - ❏ "That's a little scary about the branches being thrown in the fire!"
   - ❏ "This is a lot to digest in one sitting!"
   - ❏ "Love one another—that's what it's all about!"
   - ❏ Other_____.

2. What is Jesus saying about how a person can "bear much fruit" and have a productive life (v. 5)? Why can't a person be truly productive by him or herself?

3. What does Jesus mean when he says that he wants their joy to be "complete" (v. 11)? What does obedience to God have to do with joy that is "complete"?

4. What does Jesus say is the greatest way of showing love? How did Jesus show this kind of love to us?

5. Why is Jesus going to start referring to his disciples as "friends" instead of as "servants"? What does it mean to you that Jesus is your friend?

6. What is the greatest act of love that you have done for a friend?

7. What part of the teaching of this passage challenges you the most at this point in your life?
❏ The assumption that my life should "bear fruit."
❏ The requirement of remaining attached to Christ.
❏ The requirement to love as Christ loved.

What do you need to do to better follow this difficult teaching?

GOING DEEPER: *If your group has time and/or wants a challenge, go on to this question.*

8. Jesus says, "Greater love has no one than this, that he lay down his life for his friends" (v. 13). What is the difference between such self-sacrificing friendship and having a "martyr complex"?

CARING TIME   15 Min.
APPLY THE LESSON AND PRAY FOR ONE ANOTHER

LEADER
Encourage everyone to participate in this important time and be sure that each group member is receiving prayer support. Continue to pray for the empty chair in the closing group prayer.

Come together now for this time of caring, and help each other to have complete joy in the Lord through sharing and prayer. Begin by responding to the following questions, then share prayer requests and close with a group prayer.

1. Do you feel more like Jesus' servant or friend? What can you do in the coming week to develop your friendship with Jesus?

2. Who is in your life that you find it very difficult to love right now? How would you like the group to pray about this situation?

3. How can this group support you in your efforts to have a fruitful life? Pray for the challenges group members mentioned in question #7.

NEXT WEEK

Today we discussed Jesus' descriptive comparison of himself to a vine, on which we, his followers, are dependent branches. We were also reminded that to love each other is to obey Jesus' greatest command. In the coming week, do something special for the person you mentioned in question #2 in the Caring Time. Next week we will consider how Christ prayed both for his disciples and those believers, like us, who would come later.

NOTES ON JOHN 15:1–17

Summary: In John, Jesus uses a variety of "I am" statements to define who he is, and what his mission is. In this chapter he defines himself as being like a vine. It would have been a natural allusion in a land where wine was an important crop. The people would understand that a vine that didn't produce fruit wouldn't be worth much. They would also understand that in order to be at its most productive, a vine would have to have unproductive branches trimmed off. A branch that somehow became separated from the vine would also become useless (v. 6). This allusion was giving a message to those who were followers of Jesus. They would be facing persecution and there would be the temptation to "separate themselves from the vine." Jesus was telling them in advance that such an action would result in them being unproductive and ultimately judged by God. Only by remaining connected to Christ can a person live a productive life with the promise of eternal life to follow.

In the middle of the passage, Jesus switches to a different kind of connection image—that of friends. This is a positive companion of the more negative image of the judgment of the unproductive vine. If the disciples remain connected to Christ, they have the opportunity to consider themselves a friend of Jesus. And the really great thing about this is that Jesus is the friend par excellence. He even goes to the extent of laying down his life for his friends, the ultimate act of friendship. In this kind of friendship and love, we have an example to follow in learning what true love really is.

15:1 *I am the true vine.* The image of the vine was used to describe Israel in the Old Testament (Ps. 80:14–18; Isa. 5:1–7). But Israel did not produce the fruits God expected (Isa. 5:1–7; Matt. 21:43). Jesus transfers this image to himself. He is the "true vine" who, because he always does what pleases the Father (8:29), produces fruit for God.

15:2 *cuts off/prunes.* A gardener cuts off dead branches that do not contribute to the plant, and trims small branches so that when they grow back they might be stronger.

15:3 *clean.* This word in Greek is from the same root as that of "prunes" in verse 2. The metaphor is that of being cleansed from sin because of Jesus' death (13:10).

15:4 *bear fruit.* Although Paul uses the image of fruit to describe Christian character (Gal. 5:22–23), the fruit here probably relates to John 4:35 and 12:24 where a similar agricultural image is used to speak of the many people who would come to Christ. Just as Jesus' fruitfulness was dependent on his doing the Father's will, so the disciple's is dependent on holding on to Jesus' teaching.

15:7 *ask whatever you wish, and it will be given you.* Here the promise is in the context of spiritual fruitfulness. See also its counterpart in verse 16.

15:10 *If you obey my commands.* This is not a reversion to legalism, i.e., "If you do all the right things, I will love you." Rather it's saying that if we expect Christ's (and God's) love, then we need to give him our obedience. The commands mentioned are probably the two great commandments of loving God with all our heart, soul and mind and loving our neighbor as our self (Matt. 22:34–40; see also verse 17).

15:11 *that your joy may be complete.* God does not call us to obedience to make us miserable, but to give us a joyful, complete life (Neh. 8:10; Rom. 15:13; Gal. 5:22–23).

15:15 *friends.* The disciples' relationship with Jesus is modeled upon that of Jesus with his Father. In John 5:19–20, Jesus said the Father showed him all that he does. In the same way, Jesus has now revealed to the disciples all that he has learned from the Father.

Session 6
A Parting Prayer

SCRIPTURE JOHN 17:6–23

LAST WEEK

In last week's session we saw Jesus teaching the disciples how important it is that they, and us, remain intimately connected to him, similar to how branches are completely dependent on the vine they are connected to. We were encouraged to "remain" in Jesus and thus receive the strength and ability to "bear fruit" and love others. This week we will consider a beautiful prayer Jesus prayed for his followers, and what that prayer says about what Jesus wants for us.

ICE-BREAKER   15 Min.
Connect With Your Group

LEADER
Begin with a prayer that God will bless this time together. Choose one or two of the Ice-Breaker questions. If you have a new group member you may want to do all three.

With all of the problems in today's society, in addition to personal problems, it's always nice to know that someone is praying for you, especially when that someone is Jesus! In today's Scripture passage, Jesus prays for protection "from the evil one" and unity among believers. Take turns sharing your experiences with needing protection and finding unity.

1. When you were a child in grade school, what did you feel you needed protection from the most?
   ❏ The "monsters" under the bed.
   ❏ The school bully.
   ❏ The opposite sex.
   ❏ My parents' anger.
   ❏ Other_____.

2. What do you feel you most need protection from right now?
  ❏ Debt.
  ❏ The violence in our society.
  ❏ Unjust accusations.
  ❏ Other_____

3. With whom do you feel the greatest sense of unity right now?
  ❏ My spouse.
  ❏ A special friend.
  ❏ This group.
  ❏ Other_____.

BIBLE STUDY — 30 Min.
Read Scripture and Discuss

LEADER
Select a member of the group ahead of time to read aloud the Scripture passage. Then divide into subgroups of four or five to discuss the Questions for Interaction.

We are called to take our concerns to God in prayer, and Jesus gave us several examples of how to do that. The best-known example, of course, we call The Lord's Prayer. But here in John is another prayer of Jesus that illustrates the types of things God wants us to bring to him in prayer. Read John 17:6–23 and note the reason that unity among believers is so important.

Jesus Prays for His Disciples

6 *"I have revealed you to those whom you gave me out of the world. They were yours; you gave them to me and they have obeyed your word. ⁷Now they know that everything you have given me comes from you. ⁸For I gave them the words you gave me and they accepted them. They knew with certainty that I came from you, and they believed that you sent me. ⁹I pray for them. I am not praying for the world, but for those you have given me, for they are yours. ¹⁰All I have is yours, and all you have is mine. And glory has come to me through them. ¹¹I will remain in the world no longer, but they are still in the world, and I am coming to you. Holy Father, protect them by the power of your name—the name you gave me—so that they may be one as we are one. ¹²While I was with them, I protected them and kept them safe by that name you gave me. None has been lost except the one doomed to destruction so that Scripture would be fulfilled.*

¹³"I am coming to you now, but I say these things while I am still in the world, so that they may have the full measure of my joy within them. ¹⁴I have given them your word and the world has hated them, for they are not of the world any more than I am of the world. ¹⁵My prayer is not that you take them out of the world but that you protect them from the evil one. ¹⁶They are not of the world, even as I am not of it. ¹⁷Sanctify them by the truth; your word is truth. ¹⁸As you sent me into the world, I have sent them into the world. ¹⁹For them I sanctify myself, that they too may be truly sanctified.

²⁰"My prayer is not for them alone. I pray also for those who will believe in me through their message, ²¹that all of them may be one, Father, just as you are in me and I am in you. May they also be in us so that the world may believe that you have sent me. ²²I have given them the glory that you gave me, that they may be one as we are one: ²³I in them and you in me. May they be brought to complete unity to let the world know that you sent me and have loved them even as you have loved me.

John 17:6–23

LEADER

Refer to the Summary and Study Notes at the end of this session as needed. If 30 minutes is not enough time to answer all of the questions in this section, conclude the Bible Study by answering questions #6 and #7.

QUESTIONS FOR INTERACTION

1. Had you been one of the disciples at this time, how would you have felt upon hearing the prayer Jesus offers in verses 6–19?
   ❐ Secure and cared for.
   ❐ Humbled.
   ❐ Unworthy.
   ❐ Other_____.

2. What do you see as the most important thing Jesus is asking for on behalf of the disciples?
   ❐ Protection from the world (v. 11).
   ❐ Unity (v. 11).
   ❐ Protection from Satan (v. 15).
   ❐ That they are sanctified (made holy in their behavior—v. 17).
   ❐ Other_____.

3. Why is it significant that Jesus is not asking God to take the disciples out of the world (v. 15)? What does this mean for how Christians act in the world?

4. How are the disciples to be "sanctified"? What does it mean to be "sanctified" (see note on verse 17)?

5. Why is it important that the disciples are one (v. 11), and that the believers to come afterward (like us!) are also one (vv. 21–23)?

6. To what degree do you share the certainty that Jesus ascribes to his disciples (v. 8)?
   ❏ Completely.
   ❏ Partially.
   ❏ Not at all.

   What would help you be more certain?

7. What aspect of the world are you most feeling the need of protection from at this point in time? How can this group help you find that sense of protection?

GOING DEEPER: *If your group has time and/or wants a challenge, go on to this question.*

8. What does Jesus' call for Christian unity mean for the modern church, in the midst of our many denominations and divisions? Must an individual church or Christian compromise his or her beliefs to have this kind of unity?

CARING TIME   15 Min.
APPLY THE LESSON AND PRAY FOR ONE ANOTHER

LEADER
Be sure to save at least 15 minutes for this time of prayer and encouragement. Continue to encourage group members to invite new people to the group.

Following Jesus' example of praying to his Father for his present and future disciples, let us now gather together for a time of sharing and prayer. After responding to the following questions, share prayer requests and close in a group prayer.

1. Jesus prayed for protection of those who were closest to him. Which of your loved ones are you especially seeking protection for, and what kind of protection would you ask God to give them?

2. Consider the person on your right in this group, and the kind of concerns he or she has shared during the course of this group. What kind of protection would you ask God for on his or her behalf?

3. Take time to pray for the unity of your group and your church.

NEXT WEEK

Today we had the privilege of studying the beautiful prayer that Jesus offered on his disciples and our behalf. We were reminded of how much Jesus loves us and wants us to find peace, unity and fulfillment on this earth, even amidst the evil surrounding us. In the coming week, spend some extra time in prayer, keeping in mind Jesus' prayer as a model. Next week our focus will be the story of Jesus' arrest, as his time of suffering and dying for our sins begins.

NOTES ON JOHN 17:6–23

Summary: This material giving Jesus' extended prayer at the Last Supper has no parallel in the other Gospels. The full prayer includes petitions for himself, his disciples and future Christians. His prayer for himself, not included in this study, is really a prayer that God would be glorified through him. It reminds us of what all prayer should ultimately focus on—the glory of God. The sections where he prays for his present and future disciples focuses basically on two areas of need—protection and unity. They would need protection because Jesus knew that persecution would come. That persecution, under the likes of Nero and Domitian, lasted for a couple of hundred years, and followers of Christ faced horrendous torture and death. Paul was beheaded. Peter was crucified upside down. Under Nero Christians were sent to the lions in the coliseum and burned as human torches in Nero's gardens. However, under Nero the persecution was at least pretty much limited to Rome. Under Domitian it spread throughout the Empire.

The protection that Jesus prayed for and got for his disciples was not physical protection from death. Rather it was protection from spiritual death and the defeat of the kingdom he was establishing. Through his own coming death and resurrection, death would no longer be the final victor for people of faith, and so the threat of death would lose its sting for his disciples. And through the strength God would give Jesus' present and future disciples, their faith would be able to remain strong in the midst of persecution, and hence their witness would be effective. Thus, even in the midst of one of history's most brutal persecutions, the church grew like wildfire, spreading far into Europe and Asia.

Jesus also prayed for his followers' unity. This was important, because he knew that if the enemy could divide them, they would have a greater chance of being defeated. Indeed, in some places like Corinth, division did threaten the witness (1 Cor. 1:10–17). But the Spirit bound them together, and the church remained essentially one until the middle ages, by which time it was well established throughout the world. Today the need for unity is not over. Jesus still calls for his church to "be brought to complete unity to let the world know" that God sent him (v. 23).

17:6 they have obeyed your word. The disciples' insight that Jesus had indeed come from God (John 16:30) was the revealing factor that Jesus' mission had been successful.

17:8 They knew with certainty. This statement does not at first glance seem to describe the disciples to this point. While Peter had made a strong statement concerning Jesus and his role as Son of God and Messiah (Matt. 16:16), their confidence definitely seemed to waver. Peter cowered in fear, denying Christ after his arrest. Thomas doubted the Resurrection. And only a few women were present that Sunday morning when Christ had said he would rise again, and those women were only there because they sought to anoint the body. The confidence and certainty that Jesus speaks about may refer more to their attitude after the Resurrection and the coming of the Holy Spirit. At that point, no doubts seemed to hold them back.

17:9 I am not praying for the world. This should not be taken to mean that Jesus was unconcerned about non-believers, those who were in the world. It was because God had "so loved the world" (3:16) that Jesus had come in the first place. But right now his concern was especially for the disciples who had learned to depend on him, and whom he was getting ready to leave. **those you have given me.** Jesus' disciples are not his, but the Father's—since it is because of the Father that they have come to him (6:65).

17:11 remain in the world ... protect them. Because the world is a hostile place for the one who believes in and follows Christ (v. 14), they need protection from the world. Such words would especially have meaning to Christians later undergoing persecution for their faith. Does this protection mean that God would keep them from dying? Obviously such protection was not always there, as many Christians died for their faith. But God protected their spirit from the power of the evil one (v. 15) so that they could have eternal security. **so that they may be one as we are one.** The Spirit binds Christians together in hard times so that those times bring them together in unity instead of dividing them in dissension.

17:12 None has been lost except the one doomed. This was a reference to Judas. He had not been lost yet to physical death, which again reinforces the idea that is not what they were being protected from.

17:14 the world has hated them. The early Christians experienced much social rejection, both by Romans and Jews alike (15:18–19).

17:15 My prayer is not that you take them out of the world. In 1 Corinthians 5:9–10, Paul says that one should not avoid the immoral people of the world, because to do so would require that we leave this world. It would seem then that Christians are not called to isolate themselves from such people who are of the world, but rather we are to use the power and love of Christ to influence them. When we do that God gives us protection from the power of Satan, the evil one.

17:17 Sanctify them. This is a term that means to "make holy." To make holy, in turn, means to dedicate to God. The modern connotation of "holy" is distorted by phrases like "holier-than-thou" which implies that a holy person is a self-righteous, judgmental person. However, for people to be "sanctified" or "made holy" simply means that they are living lives dedicated to God and what God wants.

17:23 complete unity. This means unity of heart and direction. When Christians pull in different directions, it hurts the witness of Christ.

Session 7
Jesus is Arrested

Scripture John 18:1–11

LAST WEEK

The inspiring prayer that Jesus offered for his disciples and for all future believers was the topic of last week's session. We were reminded of the importance of unity among believers and how essential it is in our witness to the world—as Jesus said, "to let the world know that you sent me and have loved them even as you have loved me" (17:23). This week we turn from the words of Jesus to the drama surrounding his arrest that eventually leads to his suffering and death for our salvation.

ICE-BREAKER   15 Min.
Connect With Your Group

LEADER
After beginning with a word of prayer, introduce and welcome new group members. If there are no new members, choose one or two of the Ice-Breaker questions to get started. If there are new members, then discuss all three.

Playing "hide and seek" is always a favorite game among children. Sometimes we play it in a different way as adults! Take turns sharing some of your own experiences in life with playing "hide and seek."

1. When you were in high school, where did you and your friends go to get away from the "harassment" of parents and other adult authority figures? Who were the friends you went there with?

2. What was the situation the last time someone came looking for you?
   ❏ I did something wrong at work.
   ❏ I went back on my word with my family.
   ❏ Someone was angry and looking for someone to blame.
   ❏ Someone needed help fixing something he or she had already messed up.
   ❏ Other_____.

3. When was the last time you struck out at someone without thinking first, and then regretted it later? What happened?

BIBLE STUDY   30 Min.
READ SCRIPTURE AND DISCUSS

LEADER

Select two members of the group ahead of time to read aloud the Scripture passage. Have one person read the part of John, the narrator, and the other person read the part of Jesus. Ask the rest of the group to read the part of the officials. Then divide into subgroups of four or five to discuss the Questions for Interaction.

Jesus taught out in the open in Jerusalem, but he was never arrested because the authorities were afraid of the reaction of the crowds around him. So Judas led them to the Garden of Gethsemane, where they could arrest him at night without the crowds around him. Read John 18:1–11 and note the reaction of the soldiers to Jesus and Jesus' reaction to Peter.

Jesus Arrested

John: **18** *When he had finished praying, Jesus left with his disciples and crossed the Kidron Valley. On the other side there was an olive grove, and he and his disciples went into it. ²Now Judas, who betrayed him, knew the place, because Jesus had often met there with his disciples. ³So Judas came to the grove, guiding a detachment of soldiers and some officials from the chief priests and Pharisees. They were carrying torches, lanterns and weapons. ⁴Jesus, knowing all that was going to happen to him, went out and asked them,*

Jesus: *"Who is it you want?"*

Officials: *⁵"Jesus of Nazareth," they replied.*

Jesus: *"I am he," Jesus said.*

John: *(And Judas the traitor was standing there with them.) ⁶When Jesus said, "I am he," they drew back and fell to the ground. ⁷Again he asked them,*

Jesus: *"Who is it you want?"*

Officials:	And they said, "Jesus of Nazareth."
Jesus:	⁸"I told you that I am he," Jesus answered. "If you are looking for me, then let these men go."
John:	⁹This happened so that the words he had spoken would be fulfilled: "I have not lost one of those you gave me." ¹⁰Then Simon Peter, who had a sword, drew it and struck the high priest's servant, cutting off his right ear. (The servant's name was Malchus.)
Jesus:	¹¹Jesus commanded Peter, "Put your sword away! Shall I not drink the cup the Father has given me?"

John 18:1–11

LEADER

Refer to the Summary and Study Notes at the end of this session as needed. If 30 minutes is not enough time to answer all of the questions in this section, conclude the Bible Study by answering questions #6 and #7.

QUESTIONS FOR INTERACTION

1. What do you think would have been your strongest feeling had you been one of the disciples with Jesus at the time of his arrest?
   - ❒ Fear for my life.
   - ❒ Anger at Judas.
   - ❒ Anger at the authorities for taking Jesus in such a cowardly way.
   - ❒ Disappointment that Jesus didn't do something miraculous.
   - ❒ Other_____.

2. Why does John point out that Jesus knew what was going to happen to him (v. 4)? How does this change the impact of what happens to Jesus?

3. Why do you think that, when Jesus identifies himself, the soldiers draw back and fall to the ground?
   - ❒ Out of reverence.
   - ❒ Out of fear of his power.
   - ❒ Out of an expectation that his disciples would attack.
   - ❒ Other_____.

4. What does it say to you that Jesus spoke up at this point to protect his disciples? When were the words spoken that are quoted in verse 9?

5. What is the "cup" that Jesus refers to? Why is it necessary that he take it?

6. What enemy have you been tempted to strike violently against, as Peter struck against the high priest's slave? What do you think Jesus would say to you if you were to do so?

7. In what ways are you betraying Jesus by what you say and don't say?

GOING DEEPER: *If your group has time and/or wants a challenge, go on to this question.*

8. What does the incident of Peter striking with the sword say about how we should go about fighting for Christ and the role of physical violence?

CARING TIME 15 Min.
APPLY THE LESSON AND PRAY FOR ONE ANOTHER

LEADER
Continue to encourage group members to invite new people to the group. Remind everyone that this group is for learning and sharing, but also for reaching out to others. Close the group prayer by thanking God for each member and for this time together.

Take some time now to pray for one another, remembering how much God loves you. Begin by sharing your responses to the following questions. Then share prayer requests and close with prayer.

1. What season are you experiencing in your spiritual life right now?
   ❏ The warmth of summer.
   ❏ The dead of winter.
   ❏ The new life of spring.
   ❏ The changes of fall.

2. Where are people trying to solve conflicts by "striking with the sword" in the world today? Be in prayer that Christ will help them find a better way.

3. What "enemies" seem to be "coming for you"? How can this group help you in prayer concerning them?

NEXT WEEK

Today we considered the story of Jesus' arrest and saw how, even in the midst of this horrible betrayal, he used the situation to bring healing and hope. We were reminded that we need to ask, "What would Jesus do?" when we are fighting our battles for him. In the coming week, pray for those who have betrayed or hurt you in the past. Next week we will look at Peter's denial of Christ and the warnings we need to take to heart from his excruciating failure to stand by his Lord in a time of crisis.

NOTES ON JOHN 18:1–11

Summary: Even though Jesus knew he would be arrested as part of God's plan to redeem humanity, there are still many tragic aspects to it. It happened in the Garden of Gethsemane, a place he and his disciples had used as a safe retreat from the pressures and dangers of Jerusalem. When a place of retreat is violated, that is always sad. But this was especially so because the one who had led the soldiers to the place and betrayed this safe spot was Judas, one of the twelve disciples. Again, Jesus knew this would happen and had predicted it at the Last Supper. Still, he was one who had lived with Jesus and worked side by side with him for three years, and how could it be anything but tragic when such a friend betrays you?

However, experiencing betrayal was part of what Jesus needed to do. Hebrews tells us, "Since the children have flesh and blood, he too shared in their humanity" (Heb. 2:14). He needed to share in what it was like to be betrayed by a friend and to know no safe place, so that when these things happen to us he could understand. It's just one more way that Jesus showed how much God loves us. He didn't just take on the big pains like the Cross; he also took on what some might call the "little pains" like betrayal and rejection. We can have confidence in the love and understanding of such a Savior.

18:1 *Kidron Valley.* This valley was one of the borders of Jerusalem. During the rainy season it was a torrent, but otherwise it was dry. ***olive grove.*** Literally, "a garden." Luke 22:39 locates this on the Mount of Olives, while Matthew 26:36 and Mark 14:32 refer to it as Gethsemane. It was a place of refuge to which Jesus and the disciples often retreated during visits to Jerusalem (v. 2; Luke 22:39).

18:2 *Judas, who betrayed him.* This author gives no details about Judas' betrayal. See Luke 22:1–6,47–48 for more details.

18:3 *detachment of soldiers.* The word for "detachment" is a technical one meaning a force of 600 soldiers. Only Pilate would have the authority to dispatch these troops. This strong show of force would make sense if the Jewish authorities had told

Pilate that Jesus and the disciples were planning an insurrection, which according to John 11:48, is what the authorities feared.

18:4 *knowing all that was going to happen to him.* On at least three occasions Jesus predicted these things would happen (Matt. 16:21–23; 20:17–19; 26:2).

18:8 *let these men go.* This petition on the disciples' behalf is unique to John. It shows that even in his hour of need, Jesus was thinking of the welfare of his followers. It also shows that the disciples were in danger of arrest because of their association with Jesus. This is evident from other stories in John, such as Peter's denial (18:15–27) and the hiding of the disciples behind locked doors after the Crucifixion (20:19).

18:9 *so that the words he had spoken would be fulfilled.* This refers to John 6:39 and 17:12. This phrase is similar to the one used in John 13:18 and 15:25 when referring to Old Testament passages.

18:10 *Peter, who had a sword.* According to Luke 22:36–38, two of the disciples armed themselves with swords. These were daggers that could have been concealed easily. In John 13:37 Peter had pledged to die for Jesus. In light of the odds here, his attack could easily have caused that to happen! ***Malchus.*** The name of the servant is only mentioned here in the New Testament. Perhaps the community to which this Gospel was originally written knew him.

18:11 *Put your sword away!* In verse 36 this refusal to meet force with force is used by Jesus as a sign of the true nature of his kingdom. In Matthew's account, Jesus says, "Put your sword back in its place ... for all who draw the sword will die by the sword" (Matt. 26:52). Luke adds that Jesus healed the servant's ear (Luke 22:51). ***the cup.*** In the Old Testament, drinking "the cup" is sometimes a symbol of experiencing God's judgment and wrath against sin (Ezek. 23:32–34; Hab. 2:16). This use of the metaphor reminds us that Jesus himself will bear God's judgment against the sins of the people.

SESSION 8
PETER'S DENIALS

SCRIPTURE   JOHN 18:15–27

LAST WEEK

In last week's session we looked at the drama surrounding Jesus' arrest that eventually led to his suffering and death. We saw the reaction of the soldiers and the disciples, and how Jesus responded to them with healing and hope. This week we will consider one more difficult step along that road to death: Peter's denial of his Lord.

ICE-BREAKER 15 Min.
CONNECT WITH YOUR GROUP

LEADER
Begin by praying for your group and your time together. Choose one, two or all three of the Ice-Breaker questions. Be sure to welcome and introduce new group members.

Peter finds himself questioned about his association with Jesus in today's story. Take turns sharing your responses to the following questions that help to put you in Peter's shoes.

1. What past action or association would you have the hardest time owning up to? Why would it be hard?

2. What was your most memorable experience standing or sitting with other people around a fire?

3. When was the last time you felt like you were on the outside waiting for someone with "inside connections"? How did you feel at the time?

BIBLE STUDY
READ SCRIPTURE AND DISCUSS

30 Min.

LEADER

Ask a member of the group, selected ahead of time, to read aloud the Scripture passage. Then divide into subgroups of four or five and discuss the Questions for Interaction.

Jesus was not only betrayed by one of his disciples, but also, in his hour of need, one of his closest disciples denied that he had any connection with him. Jesus had predicted this, but that didn't make its reality any less painful. This, too, was part of what he suffered for us. Read John 18:15–27 and note the different responses to the questioning of Peter and Jesus.

The High Priest Questions Jesus

^{15}Simon Peter and another disciple were following Jesus. Because this disciple was known to the high priest, he went with Jesus into the high priest's courtyard, ^{16}but Peter had to wait outside at the door. The other disciple, who was known to the high priest, came back, spoke to the girl on duty there and brought Peter in.

^{17}"You are not one of his disciples, are you?" the girl at the door asked Peter.

He replied, "I am not."

^{18}It was cold, and the servants and officials stood around a fire they had made to keep warm. Peter also was standing with them, warming himself.

^{19}Meanwhile, the high priest questioned Jesus about his disciples and his teaching.

^{20}"I have spoken openly to the world," Jesus replied. "I always taught in synagogues or at the temple, where all the Jews come together. I said nothing in secret. ^{21}Why question me? Ask those who heard me. Surely they know what I said."

^{22}When Jesus said this, one of the officials nearby struck him in the face. "Is this the way you answer the high priest?" he demanded.

^{23}"If I said something wrong," Jesus replied, "testify as to what is wrong. But if I spoke the truth, why did you strike me?" ^{24}Then Annas sent him, still bound, to Caiaphas the high priest.

^{25}As Simon Peter stood warming himself, he was asked, "You are not one of his disciples, are you?"

He denied it, saying, "I am not."

^{26}One of the high priest's servants, a relative of the man whose ear Peter had cut off, challenged him, "Didn't I see you with him in the olive grove?" ^{27}Again Peter denied it, and at that moment a rooster began to crow.

John 18:15–27

LEADER
Refer to the Summary and Study Notes at the end of this session as needed. If 30 minutes is not enough time to answer all of the questions in this section, conclude the Bible Study by answering question #7.

QUESTIONS FOR INTERACTION

1. With whom do you identify most strongly in this story?
   - ❐ Peter, because I know what it is to turn my back on a friend.
   - ❐ The "other disciple" because I have influence in high places.
   - ❐ Jesus, because I also have been through such an interrogation.
   - ❐ One of Peter's accusers, because nobody seems to want to give me the straight story.
   - ❐ Other_____.

2. Why do Peter and the other disciple follow Jesus after he is arrested? What were they hoping to accomplish?

3. Why does Peter deny that he is one of the disciples? What is he afraid of? Why do you think the "other disciple" isn't similarly questioned?

4. What point is Jesus making to the high priest in verses 20–21? Why might the high priest *not* want to question those who heard Jesus teach in the temple?

5. What is the significance of the fact that Peter is being asked about his association with Jesus at the same time that Jesus himself is being interrogated? How do the two compare in how they deal with their interrogators?

6. Why is it pointed out that the last interrogator of Peter is a relative of the man whose ear Peter had cut off? How would that affect Peter's motivation to tell the truth?

7. In what context do you have the hardest time admitting that you are a follower of Jesus Christ? What makes it difficult for you?

GOING DEEPER: *If your group has time and/or wants a challenge, go on to this question.*

8. How would you respond if someone were to play "the Devil's Advocate" and ask, "What good would it have done at this point for Peter to admit he was a follower of Christ?"

CARING TIME 15 Min.
APPLY THE LESSON AND PRAY FOR ONE ANOTHER

LEADER

Have you started working with your group about their mission—perhaps by sharing the dream of multiplying into two groups by the end of this study of John?

Encourage and support one another now with a time of prayer, remembering that Jesus understands what you're going through. Take turns sharing your responses to the following questions before closing in prayer.

1. What is your biggest concern about the coming week?

2. What "other disciple" are you grateful for as one who has followed along with you during a tough time? Take time to thank God for this person.

3. How can this group help you to speak up more boldly in the difficult context you shared about in question #7? Take time to pray for God's strength in that context.

NEXT WEEK

Today we looked at the difficult story of Peter's denial of knowing Christ or having any connection to him whatever. We were reminded that we need God's strength and the encouragement of other believers to be able to stand up for Christ in today's world. In the coming week, ask the Holy Spirit to give you the boldness to speak up for your faith and defend Jesus' name. Next week we will look at what happened when Jesus stood before Pilate to be tried for his "crimes," and what Jesus' response to Pilate regarding his kingdom means for us today.

NOTES ON JOHN 18:15–27

Summary: Many of us have discovered that we can face almost anything if our friends stand beside us. Maybe it's a frightening report from the doctor. Maybe it's a rough time with rebellious kids. Maybe it's a time out of work. If our friends are there, encouraging us, standing with us and responding lovingly to our need, it's so much less difficult. Part of Jesus' suffering for us was that he didn't have that. His friends deserted him. Even Peter, whom he had called "the rock" denied three times that he even knew him.

At the very same time that Peter was denying Jesus because of his fear, Jesus was holding true to his message in spite of violence and threats. What he proclaimed as true, he pointed to and stood by. He did not quiver in his shoes when one of the most politically powerful men of his society accused, struck and threatened him. That Jesus showed this kind of courage reveals that the one we proclaim as Lord was not intimidated by pain and death. He was not intimidated because he knew that God would give him the victory over these forces. And the really good news is that we can have the same victory if we put our faith in him.

18:15 *another disciple.* The identity of this disciple is unknown, although some believe this is John himself. Whoever it was had some pull with the high priest, because only on this disciple's word could Peter be admitted to the high priest's courtyard. It would be hard to see how John, a fisherman from Galilee, would have such influence.

18:18 *servants and officials.* The officials were the temple police who had helped escort Jesus to the high priest, but who were not needed while he was being questioned. They would be needed again when he was escorted to the next place, and so they were now waiting.

18:20 *I have spoken openly to the world.* Jesus' teaching has been public all along. If they wanted to know what he taught, they have had ample opportunity to do so (8:43; 10:25). According to Jewish law, people were not required to testify against themselves; witnesses were required. Jesus' answer and his suggestion that they call on others who had heard what he had said (v. 21) may be his way of pointing out to the high priest that this was an illegal hearing, since there were no such witnesses present.

18:22 *struck him.* The high priest was to be spoken to with nothing but the utmost respect, however this was not always easy when the high priest did not act legally on a life and death matter. See Acts 23:3 where Paul similarly speaks against the unjust methods of the high priest.

18:26 *a relative of the man whose ear Peter had cut off.* John alone includes this detail about Peter's third accuser. Had Peter admitted his identity at this point, he would not only have risked arrest as a supporter of Jesus of Nazareth, he would have risked retaliation by this relative of Malchus (18:10).

18:27 *a rooster began to crow.* Jesus had predicted that before the rooster crowed, Peter would deny him three times (13:38).

SESSION 9
JESUS FACES PILATE

SCRIPTURE JOHN 18:28–40

LAST WEEK

Peter was put to the test in last week's story, when he was questioned about his association with Jesus. Sadly, he failed that test and denied three times that he was a disciple of the Lord. Through Peter's failure, we were reminded that we need God's strength and the encouragement of other believers to stand up for Christ. This week we will consider what happened when Jesus went before Pilate and was questioned about his "crimes." We will also discuss what his words tell us today about truth and the nature of his kingdom.

ICE-BREAKER   15 Min.
CONNECT WITH YOUR GROUP

LEADER
After beginning with a word of prayer, welcome and introduce new group members. Choose one, two or all three Ice-Breaker questions, depending on your group's needs.

Jesus says to Pilate in today's story that he was born "to testify to the truth" (v. 37). Take turns sharing your experiences and ideas regarding authority, leadership and purpose in life.

1. What was your earliest "brush with the law" or run-in with an authority figure other than your parents? What happened and how did you feel at the time?

2. If you were designated "King (or Queen) of the World," what would be your first proclamation? What would you want to immediately outlaw?

3. Some people say they were "born to be wild"; others say they were "born to shop" or "born to fish." What do you think you were born to do?

61

BIBLE STUDY
READ SCRIPTURE AND DISCUSS

30 Min.

LEADER

Select five members of the group ahead of time to read aloud the Scripture passage. Have one person read John's narration; one person read for Pilate; one person read for Jesus; two people read for the accusers; and the whole group read for the crowd. Then divide into smaller subgroups of four or five and discuss the Questions for Interaction.

The Jewish religious leadership did not have the right to execute anyone under Roman law, and they wanted Jesus executed. And so, to accomplish this, they sought to convince Pilate, the Roman governor, that Jesus was claiming to be king, which would make him guilty of sedition. In the following hearing before Pilate, Jesus responds to those charges. Read John 18:28–40 and note the conclusion that Pilate comes to regarding Jesus.

Jesus Before Pilate

John: ²⁸Then the Jews led Jesus from Caiaphas to the palace of the Roman governor. By now it was early morning, and to avoid ceremonial uncleanness the Jews did not enter the palace; they wanted to be able to eat the Passover. ²⁹So Pilate came out to them and asked,

Pilate: "What charges are you bringing against this man?"

Accusers: ³⁰"If he were not a criminal," they replied, "we would not have handed him over to you."

Pilate: ³¹Pilate said, "Take him yourselves and judge him by your own law."

Accusers: "But we have no right to execute anyone," the Jews objected.

John: ³²This happened so that the words Jesus had spoken indicating the kind of death he was going to die would be fulfilled. ³³Pilate then went back inside the palace, summoned Jesus and asked him,

Pilate: "Are you the king of the Jews?"

Jesus: ³⁴"Is that your own idea," Jesus asked, "or did others talk to you about me?"

Pilate: ³⁵"Am I a Jew?" Pilate replied. "It was your people and your chief priests who handed you over to me. What is it you have done?"

Jesus: ³⁶Jesus said, "My kingdom is not of this world. If it were, my servants would fight to prevent my arrest by the Jews. But now my kingdom is from another place."

Pilate: ³⁷"You are a king, then!" said Pilate.

Jesus: *Jesus answered, "You are right in saying I am a king. In fact, for this reason I was born, and for this I came into the world, to testify to the truth. Everyone on the side of truth listens to me."*

Pilate: *³⁸"What is truth?" Pilate asked.*

John: *With this he went out again to the Jews and said,*

Pilate: *"I find no basis for a charge against him. ³⁹But it is your custom for me to release to you one prisoner at the time of the Passover. Do you want me to release 'the king of the Jews'?"*

Crowd: *⁴⁰They shouted back, "No, not him! Give us Barabbas!"*

John: *Now Barabbas had taken part in a rebellion.*

John 18:28-40

LEADER
Refer to the Summary and Study Notes at the end of this session as needed. If 30 minutes is not enough time to answer all of the questions in this section, conclude the Bible Study by answering question #7.

QUESTIONS FOR INTERACTION

1. Had you been Jesus' defense attorney during this hearing before Pilate, what might you have done in his defense?
   - ❒ Pointed out the lack of specific charges.
   - ❒ Brought along some character witnesses.
   - ❒ Attacked the credibility of Jesus' accusers.
   - ❒ Other_____.

2. What does it say that Jesus' accusers don't really answer Pilate's question in verse 29? What does Pilate later seem to assume the charges to be (see verses 33 and 37)?

3. Why does Jesus ask the question in verse 34? Why is it important who raised the question of his kingship?

4. What does Jesus tell Pilate about the nature of his kingdom? What does he say this implies for how his kingdom is to be defended? What does this mean for those who are part of the kingdom today?

5. Why does Pilate ask, "What is truth?"
   - ❒ He really wants to know.
   - ❒ It's just a rhetorical question that has no real importance to him.
   - ❒ He's saying that truth is completely relative.
   - ❒ Other_____.

6. What would you say to someone who asked you, "What is truth?" How does your answer relate to what Jesus says in verse 37?

7. If truth were a light, how much light would you say you are getting in your life right now?
   ❒ A very small amount—Like a tiny candle in a large dark room.
   ❒ A moderate amount—Like enough light to read by.
   ❒ A large amount—Like in a well-lit room.
   ❒ An abundant amount—Like on a stage with bright stage lights.

   How do you feel about the amount of light you are getting?

GOING DEEPER: *If your group has time and/or wants a challenge, go on to this question.*

8. Why does the world so often choose the way of Barabbas, the violent rebel, over the way of Jesus?

CARING TIME   15 Min.
APPLY THE LESSON AND PRAY FOR ONE ANOTHER

LEADER
Have you identified someone in the group that could be a leader for a new small group when your group divides? How could you encourage and mentor that person?

For us to grow as Christians and bring God's kingdom to every heart we need support and encouragement. This is your time to give that to each other. Share your responses to the following questions before closing in prayer.

1. Thank God for the truth that has come into your life, as you shared about in question #7. Thank God also for those special people who have conveyed that truth to you.

2. Where do you see people right now wanting to change the world in the rebellious spirit of Barabbas? Add these people to your prayer list for today.

3. In what area of your life would you most like Jesus to help you see the truth more clearly? Pray for this enlightenment.

NEXT WEEK

Today we watched and listened as Jesus stood before Pilate and was questioned about his "crimes." We saw Jesus take this opportunity to talk about the truth and how his kingdom "is not of this world" (v. 36). In the coming week, pray that the Holy Spirit will always help you to discern the truth and avoid being deceived by the world and Satan's false promises. Next week we will look at the crucifixion of Jesus and what his indescribable suffering and death means for us and for our salvation.

NOTES ON JOHN 18:28–40

Summary: The injustice of Jesus' arrest is shown by the fact that there wasn't any real clarity as to what he had done wrong. The Jewish religious authorities, whose complaints initiated the arrest, were most upset because he claimed to be the Son of God, which they considered to be blasphemy (Matt. 26:62–66). However, they dared not bring such a religious charge before the Romans, who simply wouldn't have cared about such a claim. That's why, in this story from John, the authorities are evasive when asked what he was to be charged with (vv. 29–30). All of the other Gospels say that the religious leaders officially charged Jesus with claiming to be a king, and in this story from John that seems to be the concern of Pilate (vv. 33–37). However, Pilate finds no evidence that Jesus is seeking a kingship that is in conflict with Roman authority (v. 38).

Why then was he crucified? It seems that it happened because the religious leaders were able to turn so much popular sentiment against him, that Pilate feared what might happen if he didn't execute him. In other words, he was crucified not because he had done anything punishable by crucifixion under Roman law, but rather he was crucified for political expediency. As such, Jesus experienced what it was to be a victim of injustice. When we experience injustice in this world, we can be comforted in part by knowing that God, through Jesus Christ, understands what that is like. But we can also know that through Christ and his victory over death and evil, such injustice will be defeated in favor of a new creation in which there will be neither crying, death or pain (Rev. 21:1–4).

18:28 *palace.* The Roman seat of power over Judea was located at Caesarea (Acts 23:33–35). However, this "palace" was Pilate's temporary residence in Jerusalem, a building Herod the Great had erected as a home for himself years before. *early morning.* Jesus' trial before the high priest was either late at night or very early in the morning. The trial before Pilate probably began around 6–7 A.M., since the Roman courts began early. *to avoid ceremonial uncleanness.* Rabbinic tradition taught that Gentile homes were unclean, defiling any Jew who entered one for seven days. **The Passover.** According to the chronology of this Gospel, the Passover would be observed that evening. Any Jew ritually defiled would have to wait a month to commemorate this feast.

18:31 *judge him by your own law.* Pilate's contempt for the Jews is seen throughout this story. He knew that they had already tried Jesus or they would not have brought him. His remark is a rebuke to their attempt to rush him into passing sentence. *we have no right to execute anyone.* This is debated, since the Sanhedrin did have extensive powers, but the fact that the Roman Empire held on tightly to the sole right to pass judgment on cases involving capital punishment speaks in defense of this statement. The only exception to this prohibition was if a Gentile entered the temple.

18:32 *so that the words Jesus had spoken ... would be fulfilled.* Jesus used the metaphor of being "lifted up" as a means of describing his death (3:14; 12:32–33). The Jewish method of killing an offender would have been stoning (Acts 7:58), but the Roman method of crucifixion fulfills the metaphor.

18:33 *Are you the king of the Jews?* The Jewish authorities do not specify this charge in John's account. They do, however, in Luke's account (Luke 23:1–2). All of the Gospel accounts report that Pilate asked if Jesus was the king of the Jews. Such a claim constituted the formal charge the Jewish religious leaders were bringing against Jesus, representing him as a threat to Roman rule (vv. 34–35).

18:36 *"My kingdom is not of this world."* Jesus mitigates any concern over sedition by specifically saying that because his kingdom is not of this world his disciples are not physically fighting to establish it.

18:37 *"You are right in saying I am a king."* Compare this to Jesus' response, as recorded in all three of the Synoptic Gospels: "Yes, it is as you say" (Matt. 27:11; Mark 15:2; Luke 23:3).

18:39 *your custom.* This is unknown outside of the New Testament. It may have been a local custom during Pilate's governorship, as an attempt to placate the Jews. *'the king of the Jews.'* This is a jibe at the authorities. He is willing to release the one claiming to be their king, for he sees no threat at all in him.

18:40 *Barabbas.* The irony here is that his name means "son of the father." Luke 23:19 says he was an insurrectionist and murderer.

SESSION 10
THE CRUCIFIXION

SCRIPTURE   JOHN 19:16–37

LAST WEEK

In last week's session we discussed what happened when Jesus went before Pilate to answer for his "crimes." We saw him take this difficult situation, and in spite of the injustice of it all, use it to communicate his ideas about truth and the nature of his kingdom. We were reminded that we need to seek the truth at all times and know that we are part of a heavenly kingdom, not an earthly one. This week we will consider the end result of that legal process, Jesus' death on a cruel cross, and reflect on what that death means for us.

ICE-BREAKER   15 Min.
CONNECT WITH YOUR GROUP

LEADER
Begin with a word of prayer and then discuss one, two or all three of the Ice-Breaker questions. Remember to stick closely to the three-part agenda and the time allowed for each segment.

Each of us has unique experiences that make us who God wants us to be and help us to fulfill God's plan for our life. Jesus' life experiences helped to make him the perfect sacrifice for our sins. Take turns sharing some of your experiences and thoughts by answering the following questions.

1. When you were in grade school, how did you and your siblings (or friends) divide up things or privileges that all of you wanted?
   ❏ The "top dog" ruled.
   ❏ We chose a number and whoever was the closest won.
   ❏ We took turns.
   ❏ Other _____.

   Did you think your system was fair?

2. When you were a child, who besides your own parents was like a parent to you? What made you feel this way about this person? 3 If you were to choose one sign to be placed over you when you die, what would the sign say?

BIBLE STUDY 30 Min.
Read Scripture and Discuss

Leader

Ask a member of the group, selected ahead of time, to read aloud the Scripture passage. Then discuss the Questions for Interaction, dividing into subgroups of four or five.

Although Pilate insisted that he found no crime in Jesus worthy of death, he gave in to the demands of the crowd and allowed Jesus to be crucified. Crucifixion was a horrid way to die. It was slow and painful. It was intended to be a way where all persons passing by could look up and see the power of Rome and what happens to those who defy Rome. But in this case, it became a way for all persons to look up and see the love of God, and what God was willing to do for all persons who would believe. Read John 19:16–37 and note how Scripture is fulfilled.

The Crucifixion

19 *Finally Pilate handed him over to them to be crucified. So the soldiers took charge of Jesus.* ^{17}*Carrying his own cross, he went out to the place of the Skull (which in Aramaic is called Golgotha).* ^{18}*Here they crucified him, and with him two others–one on each side and Jesus in the middle.*

^{19}*Pilate had a notice prepared and fastened to the cross. It read: JESUS OF NAZARETH, THE KING OF THE JEWS.* ^{20}*Many of the Jews read this sign, for the place where Jesus was crucified was near the city, and the sign was written in Aramaic, Latin and Greek.* ^{21}*The chief priests of the Jews protested to Pilate, "Do not write 'The King of the Jews,' but that this man claimed to be king of the Jews."*

^{22}*Pilate answered, "What I have written, I have written."*

^{23}*When the soldiers crucified Jesus, they took his clothes, dividing them into four shares, one for each of them, with the undergarment remaining. This garment was seamless, woven in one piece from top to bottom.*

^{24}*"Let's not tear it," they said to one another. "Let's decide by lot who will get it."*

This happened that the scripture might be fulfilled which said,

> *"They divided my garments among them*
> *and cast lots for my clothing."*

So this is what the soldiers did.

^{25}Near the cross of Jesus stood his mother, his mother's sister, Mary the wife of Clopas, and Mary Magdalene. ^{26}When Jesus saw his mother there, and the disciple whom he loved standing nearby, he said to his mother, "Dear woman, here is your son," ^{27}and to the disciple, "Here is your mother." From that time on, this disciple took her into his home.

^{28}Later, knowing that all was now completed, and so that the Scripture would be fulfilled, Jesus said, "I am thirsty." ^{29}A jar of wine vinegar was there, so they soaked a sponge in it, put the sponge on a stalk of the hyssop plant, and lifted it to Jesus' lips. ^{30}When he had received the drink, Jesus said, "It is finished." With that, he bowed his head and gave up his spirit.

^{31}Now it was the day of Preparation, and the next day was to be a special Sabbath. Because the Jews did not want the bodies left on the crosses during the Sabbath, they asked Pilate to have the legs broken and the bodies taken down. ^{32}The soldiers therefore came and broke the legs of the first man who had been crucified with Jesus, and then those of the other.

^{33}But when they came to Jesus and found that he was already dead, they did not break his legs. ^{34}Instead, one of the soldiers pierced Jesus' side with a spear, bringing a sudden flow of blood and water. ^{35}The man who saw it has given testimony, and his testimony is true. He knows that he tells the truth, and he testifies so that you also may believe. ^{36}These things happened so that the scripture would be fulfilled: "Not one of his bones will be broken," ^{37}and, as another scripture says, "They will look on the one they have pierced."

John 19:16–37

LEADER

Refer to the Summary and Study Notes at the end of this session as needed. If 30 minutes is not enough time to answer all of the questions in this section, conclude the Bible Study by answering questions #6 and #7.

QUESTIONS FOR INTERACTION

1. If were you working on the sound track for a movie that included this scene, what kind of music would you choose as a background for these events?
   - ❐ Sad and mournful.
   - ❐ Bold, dramatic and stirring.
   - ❐ Discordant, like forces clashing.
   - ❐ Other_____.

2. Why do you think Pilate wanted to stick with the words of his original sign, instead of the words that the chief priests asked for?

3. What does it suggest to you that the soldiers divided up Jesus' clothing while he was dying on the cross?
❒ They were hardened to death.
❒ They were trying not to watch what was going on.
❒ They were just trying to provide for their families.
❒ Other_____.

4. Why does Jesus direct his mother and John ("the disciple whom he loved") toward each other? How would you have felt about this had you been Mary? Had you been John?

5. When Jesus says, "It is finished," what is he saying is finished? Is it a cry of despair, relief or fulfillment (see note on v. 30)?

6. Who have you become closer to because of a shared hour of grief, such as John and Mary experienced? Was this closeness maintained?

7. In your own relationship to Jesus Christ right now, which of the characters in this story are you most like?
❒ The chief priests, insisting he is not the King.
❒ The soldiers gambling for his clothes, trying not to think about it.
❒ John and Mary, feeling his pain together.
❒ "The man who saw it" (John), because I know it's true.

GOING DEEPER: *If your group has time and/or wants a challenge, go on to this question.*

8. Why is there so much emphasis in this passage on the fulfillment of Scripture (vv. 24,36–37)? What difference does it make that what happened during Jesus' suffering and death had been referred to ahead of time in Scripture?

CARING TIME — 15 Min.
APPLY THE LESSON AND PRAY FOR ONE ANOTHER

Begin this Caring Time by sharing your responses to the following questions. Then take some time to share prayer requests and pray for one another.

LEADER

Conclude the group prayer today by reading Isaiah 53:4–5: *Surely he took up our infirmities and carried our sorrows, yet we considered him stricken by God, smitten by him, and afflicted. But he was pierced for our transgressions, he was crushed for our iniquities; the punishment that brought us peace was upon him, and by his wounds we are healed.*

1. What would you like to thank God for in the relationship you talked about in question #6? Make sure you include this in your prayer time.

2. For what do you "thirst" right now in your spiritual life? Have everyone in the group pray for the person on his or her right, and what it is they "thirst" for.

3. Take time to pray for a strengthening of your relationship to Jesus Christ. In doing so, remember what you shared in question #7.

NEXT WEEK

Today we watched as Jesus' unconditional love for us led him to the ultimate sacrifice—a gruesome death by crucifixion. We were reminded how everything that happened was a fulfillment of Scripture and showed that Jesus was truly the Messiah that had been promised. In the coming week, write a special thank you to Jesus for all he went through for your salvation on his road to Calvary. Next week we will look at the first of several exciting, post-Resurrection stories in John, giving us cause for hope and joy.

NOTES ON JOHN 19:16–37

Summary: Never has a symbol been turned around so completely. Before Jesus Christ, the cross was the symbol of infamy and defeat. It was the end result for criminals who defied Rome and had the bad luck to get caught. It was a bloody and horrible way to die—so bad that it was kept outside the city where respectable citizens didn't have to see it if they didn't want to. The cross was part of that whole symbolism of death and criminality. And then Christ died on it, and bought freedom for all who would believe from the power of death. Today the cross is a symbol of faith and the victory of hope over death. It adorns elaborate cathedrals, and is worn around the necks of rich and poor alike. The cross has become one of the most recognized positive symbols in our culture.

As the cross has turned around as a symbol, so also the one who believes can turn their life around through Jesus Christ. That is what Christ seeks to do with all of us, and it is why he went to that Cross. He wanted to defeat every barrier that could come between a positive life of faith in him and us, whether it is the barrier of death or the barrier of a negative image such as the cross—and many people—have. Christ breaks down all the barriers. That is why the story of an instrument of death is now called Good News.

19:17 *Carrying his own cross.* As part of the humiliation before crucifixion, condemned prisoners had to carry at least the crossbar of the cross to the site of their execution, where the vertical bars were normally permanently installed. *place of the Skull.* No definitive reason has been given as to why this place had this name, although there is a hill in Jerusalem today that has the appearance of a skull. It may have been a common place for execution.

19:19 *Pilate had a notice prepared and fastened to the cross.* There is no evidence that this was a normal practice, although some prisoners were required to wear signs listing their crimes around their necks. **JESUS OF NAZARETH, THE KING OF THE JEWS.** The sign listed the name and origin of Jesus, as well as the crime for which he was convicted.

19:20 *Aramaic, Latin and Greek.* These were the three common languages of the area. Jews from outside of Palestine would not necessarily have been able to read Aramaic (the local language of the area), nor Latin (the official language of the empire), but all would have known Greek, since that was the common trade language.

19:21 *The chief priests ... protested.* All along the opposition had been upset at Jesus' claims. They were upset that Pilate's sign left the matter uncertain to those who would read it as to whether Jesus only claimed this title, or if he was really the Messiah whom Rome had defeated.

19:25 *his mother, his mother's sister, Mary the wife of Clopas, and Mary Magdalene.* It appears there were four women present: Jesus' mother, his aunt, Mary, the wife of Clopas and Mary Magdalene. Nothing is known of Mary the wife of Clopas, except that she may have been the wife of the Cleopas, who witnessed the risen Christ on the road to Emmaus (Luke 24:18). Mary Magdalene does not appear earlier in this Gospel. Particularly touching, though, is the presence of Jesus' mother, watching her own son die a horrible death normally reserved for criminals. Simeon had warned her, "a sword will pierce your own soul too" (Luke 2:35).

19:26 *the disciple whom he loved.* This would no doubt be John himself. It appears that by this time Joseph, Mary's husband, was dead. As the oldest son, Jesus would have assumed the responsibility of caring for his mother, and Jesus is transferring this responsibility to John.

19:29 *wine vinegar.* This was cheap wine. It was probably on the scene for the entertainment of the soldiers as they waited for the process of crucifixion to accomplish its course. It would have done little for his thirst, and its bitterness would have been symbolic of the overall bitterness of the experience.

19:30 *"It is finished."* Given the emphasis in this Gospel on Jesus doing the Father's work, it is clear that by this Jesus is saying his work has been accomplished. *gave up his spirit.* Even though he was on the cross, his death was a voluntary action on his part. Others did not take his life away; he sacrificed it freely (10:18).

19:31 *the Jews did not want the bodies left on the crosses.* Although the Roman custom was to leave the bodies on the crosses as a warning for criminals, Jewish law forbade bodies hung on a tree from remaining overnight (Deut. 21:22–23). *the legs broken.* By pressing their weight on their legs, victims could ease some of the pressure upon their arms and chest, making breathing easier. However, once their legs were broken, this relief was no longer possible, and death by suffocation and shock would come quickly.

19:34 *pierced Jesus' side.* This would ensure that he was indeed dead. It counters the claim some have made that Jesus' apparent resurrection was due to the fact that he never really died in the first place.

19:35 *The man who saw it.* This might be John the apostle who either wrote this Gospel, or at least whose testimony guided the writing of this Gospel.

19:36 *Not one of his bones will be broken.* From the beginning of this Gospel, the ministry of Jesus has been pictured in terms of the Passover lamb (1:29; 6:4). One of the requirements of these lambs was that their bones should not be broken (Ex. 12:46).

Session 11
The Empty Tomb

Scripture John 20:1–18

LAST WEEK

Jesus' death on a cruel cross, and what that death means for us, was our topic for discussion in last week's session. We were reminded of Jesus' amazing love for us as we thought about the incredible ordeal he went through. The most vital thing, however, is that his death was not the end of the story. So this week we will take a look at the empty tomb, which his disciples discovered on the third day after Jesus' death, and we will look at the hope and joy that empty tomb brings.

ICE-BREAKER   15 Min.
Connect With Your Group

LEADER
Begin by praying for your group and your time together. Choose, one, two or all three Ice-Breaker questions, depending on your group's needs.

Tears of sadness and grief turn into tears of joy in today's story when Mary Magdalene discovers her Lord is alive! Take turns sharing about times you cried tears of joy or sadness.

1. When was the last time you were moved to tears due to happiness and joy?

2. When you were a teenager, what most frequently brought you to tears?
   ❏ Fighting with a parent or sibling.
   ❏ Trouble with the opposite sex.
   ❏ Sad movies or songs.
   ❏ Failure at some task or school subject.
   ❏ Other_____.

3. What is most likely to bring you to tears of sadness today?

BIBLE STUDY
READ SCRIPTURE AND DISCUSS

30 Min.

LEADER
Select a member of the group ahead of time to read aloud the Scripture passage. Then discuss the Questions for Interaction, dividing into groups of four or five.

Jesus' death temporarily crushed the spirits of his disciples. But this did not keep at least one woman from being present shortly after his resurrection. Actually, Mary Magdalene didn't come to the tomb expecting a resurrection. She came simply to perform an act of love, to do the preparations of the body that could not have been done earlier because of the Sabbath. However, because of her desire to perform this act of love, she was there at history's pivotal moment. Read John 20:1–18 and note the disciples' reaction to Mary's announcement.

The Empty Tomb

20 [1] Early on the first day of the week, while it was still dark, Mary Magdalene went to the tomb and saw that the stone had been removed from the entrance. [2] So she came running to Simon Peter and the other disciple, the one Jesus loved, and said, "They have taken the Lord out of the tomb, and we don't know where they have put him!"

[3] So Peter and the other disciple started for the tomb. [4] Both were running, but the other disciple outran Peter and reached the tomb first. [5] He bent over and looked in at the strips of linen lying there but did not go in. [6] Then Simon Peter, who was behind him, arrived and went into the tomb. He saw the strips of linen lying there, [7] as well as the burial cloth that had been around Jesus' head. The cloth was folded up by itself, separate from the linen. [8] Finally the other disciple, who had reached the tomb first, also went inside. He saw and believed. [9] (They still did not understand from Scripture that Jesus had to rise from the dead.)

[10] Then the disciples went back to their homes, [11] but Mary stood outside the tomb crying. As she wept, she bent over to look into the tomb [12] and saw two angels in white, seated where Jesus' body had been, one at the head and the other at the foot.

[13] They asked her, "Woman, why are you crying?"

"They have taken my Lord away," she said, "and I don't know where they have put him." [14] At this, she turned around and saw Jesus standing there, but she did not realize that it was Jesus.

[15] "Woman," he said, "why are you crying? Who is it you are looking for?"

Thinking he was the gardener, she said, "Sir, if you have carried him away, tell me where you have put him, and I will get him."

[16] Jesus said to her, "Mary."

She turned toward him and cried out in Aramaic, "Rabboni!" (which means Teacher).

[17]Jesus said, "Do not hold on to me, for I have not yet returned to the Father. Go instead to my brothers and tell them, 'I am returning to my Father and your Father, to my God and your God.'"

[18]Mary Magdalene went to the disciples with the news: "I have seen the Lord!" And she told them that he had said these things to her.

John 20:1–18

QUESTIONS FOR INTERACTION

LEADER
Refer to the Summary and Study Notes at the end of this session as needed. If 30 minutes is not enough time to answer all of the questions in this section, conclude the Bible Study by answering questions #6 and #7.

1. What surprises you the most in this story?
   ❒ That none of the men went to the tomb with Mary in the first place.
   ❒ That Mary assumed the body had been stolen.
   ❒ That the disciples still didn't understand the prophecies of Scripture.
   ❒ That Mary didn't recognize Jesus at first in the garden.
   ❒ Other_____.

2. Why do you think the "other disciple" hesitated to go in the tomb, even though he got there first?
   ❒ Fear of death or "ghosts."
   ❒ Fear of the soldiers he assumed had taken the body.
   ❒ Fear of being disappointed again.
   ❒ Other_____.

3. What was the significance of the fact that the grave clothes were so neatly placed?

4. Why do you think Mary didn't recognize Jesus at first?
   ❒ His body had changed.
   ❒ She wasn't expecting him to be alive.
   ❒ She was not thinking clearly or focusing well.
   ❒ Other_____.

5. Why does Jesus tell Mary not to hold on to him?
   ❒ He had places to go.
   ❒ He didn't want her to get too attached, since he would be leaving.
   ❒ Other_____.

6. What are you trying to hold on to that Jesus is calling you to let go of, so his work can go on in your life?

7. In terms of this story, where are you right now in relation to the resurrection of Jesus Christ?
- ❏ Standing at a distance, afraid to check it out (v. 5).
- ❏ Seeing the evidence, but believing the worst (vv. 2,13).
- ❏ Believing, but not fully understanding (vv. 8–9).
- ❏ Joyful over the Resurrection, and needing to talk about it (v. 18).

GOING DEEPER: *If your group has time and/or wants a challenge, go on to this question.*

8. Why is the Resurrection so hard for many to believe? What might you say to a skeptic?

CARING TIME   15 Min.
APPLY THE LESSON AND PRAY FOR ONE ANOTHER

LEADER

Conclude the prayer time today by asking God for guidance in determining the future mission and outreach of this group.

Take time to pray for one another and support one another, remembering the victory Jesus has over death and sin through his glorious resurrection. Respond to the following questions before closing in prayer.

1. Who do you need to pray for that they might fully appreciate the reality of "the empty tomb"?

2. Pray for God's strength to let go of whatever you mentioned in question #6 that is holding you back from accomplishing God's work in your life.

3. Pray for the person on your right that he or she will have a deeper appreciation of the Resurrection in their life.

> **NEXT WEEK**
>
> Today our tears of sadness turned to joy, along with Mary Magdalene, as we considered the resurrection of Jesus and the hope of forgiveness and eternal life that brings. We were reminded to let go of earthly fears and turn them into faith that believes in miracles. In the coming week, share with someone who is grieving the hope and joy of the Resurrection. Next week we will look at the story of one who doubted that Resurrection, and the challenge his story presents for us today.

NOTES ON JOHN 20:1–18

Summary: There couldn't be a more difficult thing a person might have to do than to prepare a loved one's body for burial. In our society, of course, professionals who are trained for the task, and who generally do not have a personal relationship with the person who died, take care of all this. Mary Magdalene did not have the advantage of this modern convenience. Why was she the one selected to do this task that was normally done by family members? Why wasn't Jesus' mother or James involved? Did Mary Magdalene just decide to do this on her own, or did someone select her? We don't know. However, we can be sure that it was difficult. Still, Mary Magdalene did not put off this difficult task. Our text tells us that she went to the tomb on the first day of the week "while it was still dark." That was pretty much as early as she could have done it. She could not have done it on the Sabbath, and the Sabbath lasted until sundown Saturday night. Then it would have been too dark. So she went at a time when she could do this task with the first rays of the morning's light.

What Mary found totally dumbfounded her. The tomb was empty! For her that could mean but one thing. She had seen him die, so she "knew" he could not walk away on his own. Someone must have taken the body! The truth dawned on her only slowly. Who could blame her? Resurrection from the dead is not something one normally expects! But that it happened is what makes this a pivotal event in human history. No longer would death have the last word. Jesus Christ, the Son of God, had opened the door to life beyond death. And that was also the event that turned the discouraged bunch of disciples into a dynamic band that spread throughout the world.

20:1 *the first day of the week.* This was Sunday. ***Mary Magdalene.*** Mary is mentioned in all four Gospel accounts of the Resurrection. Luke 8:2 says that she was one of several women who traveled with the disciples. ***stone.*** This account of the burial of Jesus does not mention that it was sealed with a large stone (Matt. 27:60; Mark 15:46).

20:2 *we don't know where.* All other accounts mention that there was more than one woman who came to the tomb that morning, and while John mentions only Mary Magdalene, this "we" may be an acknowledgment that others were involved.

20:5–7 *strips of linen/burial cloth.* Grave robbers, in search of treasure entombed with the corpse, would either have taken the body still wrapped up, or scattered the strips as they tore them off. The fact that the clothes were neatly laid by was one of the evidences that led the "other disciple" to faith (v. 8).

20:12 *two angels in white.* The Gospels differ on whether there was one "man" (Mark), or an angel (Matthew), or two "men" (Luke) present. This is not so unusual. In Scripture, angels are often mistaken for men (Gen. 18:1–15; 19:1–22; Judg. 6:11–24; Heb. 13:2).

20:14 *she did not realize that it was Jesus.* Whether she was blinded by her intense grief or there was some type of transformation in Jesus' appearance that caused Mary's lack of recognition is not known.

20:15 *gardener.* The tomb was located in a garden owned by Joseph (19:41). It would not be unlikely that as an aristocratic member of the Sanhedrin he would employ a gardener to care for his property.

20:16 *"Mary."* When Jesus speaks Mary's name she immediately recognizes him, thus proving her discipleship. ***Aramaic.*** This was the local language of Jews from Galilee and Judea. ***Rabboni.*** Literally, "my teacher." This is not only a title of respect for Jesus, but also one that shows Mary's submission and love for him.

20:17 *Do not hold on to me.* We need not think Jesus refused to allow her to touch him at all, but that, after Mary had expressed the joy and relief she would feel at seeing him, he simply told her that all was not finished yet.

SESSION 12
DOUBTING THOMAS

SCRIPTURE JOHN 20:19–31

LAST WEEK

"I have seen the Lord!" was Mary Magdalene's joyful cry in last week's story of the empty tomb and the resurrection of Jesus. We also saw the difficulty the first disciples had with letting go of earthly expectations and accepting the possibility that Jesus could have risen from the dead. This week we will take a look at one of the disciples who had an especially hard time believing and whose first reaction to this good news was very skeptical—Thomas. In his story we will look for our own.

ICE-BREAKER   15 Min.
CONNECT WITH YOUR GROUP

LEADER
Begin with a prayer that God will bless this time together. Choose one, two or all three of the Ice-Breaker questions, depending on your group's needs.

As we grow older, many of us learn that things are not always as they seem and promises are often not kept. We become more and more skeptical as we experience people and things that fail us. Take turns sharing your unique life experiences with being a "doubting Thomas."

1. When you were a child or adolescent, who do you remember preying upon your gullibility? What "whopper" did this person try to get you to swallow? When he or she told you the truth, how quickly did you believe them?

2. Who do you have the hardest time believing today?
  ❏ Politicians.
  ❏ Sales people.
  ❏ A family member.
  ❏ News reporters.
  ❏ Other _____.

3. What modern report whose credibility has been questioned do you most wish you could have seen for yourself?
  ❏ The assassination of JFK.
  ❏ The "alien landing" in Roswell, New Mexico.
  ❏ The death of Elvis.
  ❏ Other_____.

BIBLE STUDY 30 Min.
Read Scripture and Discuss

LEADER

Ask three members of the group, selected ahead of time, to read aloud the Scripture passage. Have one person read the part of the narrator, John; one person read for Jesus; one person read for Thomas; and the rest of the group read the part of the disciples. Then divide into subgroups of four or five and discuss the Questions for Interaction.

Jesus' resurrection was such an incredible event that it was natural not everyone would accept it readily. The best-known story of one who took the first reports with at least a "grain of salt" is that of Thomas. Like a modern scientist, he was hesitant to believe in something he couldn't see and touch. But Jesus taught him a lesson about what it means to believe in something that can't be seen. Read John 20:19–31 and note Jesus' response to Thomas when he does believe.

Jesus Appears to His Disciples

John: ¹⁹*On the evening of that first day of the week, when the disciples were together, with the doors locked for fear of the Jews, Jesus came and stood among them and said,*

Jesus: *"Peace be with you!"*

John: ²⁰*After he said this, he showed them his hands and side. The disciples were overjoyed when they saw the Lord.* ²¹*Again Jesus said,*

Jesus: *"Peace be with you! As the Father has sent me, I am sending you."*

John: ²²*And with that he breathed on them and said,*

Jesus:	"Receive the Holy Spirit. ²³If you forgive anyone his sins, they are forgiven; if you do not forgive them, they are not forgiven."
John:	²⁴Now Thomas (called Didymus), one of the Twelve, was not with the disciples when Jesus came. ²⁵So the other disciples told him,
Disciples:	"We have seen the Lord!"
John:	But he said to them,
Thomas:	"Unless I see the nail marks in his hands and put my finger where the nails were, and put my hand into his side, I will not believe it."
John:	²⁶A week later his disciples were in the house again, and Thomas was with them. Though the doors were locked, Jesus came and stood among them and said,
Jesus:	"Peace be with you!"
John:	²⁷Then he said to Thomas,
Jesus:	"Put your finger here; see my hands. Reach out your hand and put it into my side. Stop doubting and believe."
John:	²⁸Thomas said to him,
Thomas:	"My Lord and my God!"
John:	²⁹Then Jesus told him,
Jesus:	"Because you have seen me, you have believed; blessed are those who have not seen and yet have believed."
John:	³⁰Jesus did many other miraculous signs in the presence of his disciples, which are not recorded in this book. ³¹But these are written that you may believe that Jesus is the Christ, the Son of God, and that by believing you may have life in his name.

John 20:19–31

QUESTIONS FOR INTERACTION

LEADER
Refer to the Summary and Study Notes at the end of this session as needed. If 30 minutes is not enough time to answer all of the questions in this section, conclude the Bible Study by answering questions #6 and #7.

1. What is the closest you have come to having friends ask you to believe an incredible report like Thomas was asked to believe? How did you react? Were you too skeptical, too gullible or "just right"?

2. What would you say was the predominant mood of the disciples prior to Jesus entering the locked room? How does what Jesus says and does address that mood?

3. Why does Jesus breathe on the disciples? What effect does it have when he does so (see note on verse 22)?

4. What do you think was the reason behind Thomas not believing the other disciples when they told him of the Resurrection?
   ❏ Scientific skepticism.
   ❏ The caution of one afraid to hope.
   ❏ A self-protective reaction of one who didn't want to be gullible.
   ❏ Other_____.

5. How do you think Thomas felt after Jesus had him touch his hands and side, and said what he did about believing? How do you think this incident affected his life from this point on?

6. When have you reacted to something with the skepticism of Thomas? Were you able to move past that skepticism? What helped you do so?

7. What has Jesus done in your life that you could point others to so they might "believe that Jesus is the Christ" and "have life in his name" (v. 31)?

GOING DEEPER: *If your group has time and/or wants a challenge, go on to this question.*

8. Do Jesus' words to Thomas mean that it is always wrong to doubt? When is doubt a natural caution through which one must pass, and when is it something to be condemned?

CARING TIME   15 Min.
APPLY THE LESSON AND PRAY FOR ONE ANOTHER

LEADER

Following the Caring Time, discuss with your group how they would like to celebrate the last session next week. Also, discuss the possibility of splitting into two groups and continuing with another study.

Remembering the resurrection power of Jesus, go to him now in a time of sharing and prayer. After responding to the following questions, share prayer requests and close in a group prayer.

1. How would you describe your spiritual life this past week?
   - ❏ Full of doubt.
   - ❏ Increasing in doubt.
   - ❏ Full of faith.
   - ❏ Increasing in faith.
   - ❏ Half and half.
   - ❏ Other_____.

2. What doubt are you struggling with right now? Pray that God will help you with it.

3. In what area of your life do you need Christ's words "Peace be with you" to comfort you? Pray for the person on your left in relation to this need.

NEXT WEEK

Today we studied the story of doubting Thomas, the disciple who could not believe that Jesus was alive until he saw for himself the wounds in his hands and side. We were reminded of the promise that Jesus gave when he said, "Blessed are those who have not seen and yet have believed" (v. 29). In the coming week, reach out to someone who is struggling with accepting Jesus and pray that the Holy Spirit would open his or her eyes to the truth. Next week we will look at the inspiring story of how Jesus reinstated Peter to leadership after his denials, and we will meditate on what this means for us in the midst of our moral failures.

NOTES ON JOHN 20:19–31

Summary: One thing that seems obvious from Scripture is that the disciples never really understood what Jesus had told them about his coming death and resurrection until sometime after it happened. He had said, "The Son of Man will be betrayed to the chief priests and the teachers of the law. They will condemn him to death and will turn him over to the Gentiles to be mocked and flogged and crucified. On the third day he will be raised to life" (Matt. 20:18–19). And yet, in spite of this advance word, they were surprised all along the way. When Jesus rose from the dead, none of them were there to greet him, and the women only came along later to anoint the body. Even when they saw him, they couldn't let go and believe! Luke says that all the disciples doubted when they first saw him (Luke 24:37–39), and John points out that they all had to see his hands and side to be convinced it was really him (v. 20). Why then do we single out Thomas as the doubter who didn't have enough faith? None of them had much faith or they would have believed Jesus' promise, and they would have been expecting its fulfillment!

20:19 *fear of the Jews.* In spite of Jesus' words in John 14:27, the disciples were afraid that the authorities, who had been successful in having Jesus killed, might now turn on them. ***Jesus came.*** Nothing is said about how Jesus came to be among them, but the implication of the locked doors appears to be that Jesus simply appeared with them (v. 26; Luke 24:31). ***Peace be with you!*** This is repeated in verse 21 and in the appearance a week later in verse 26. The promise of peace was given in John 14:27 and 16:33. It sums up the blessings and fullness of the new covenant that Jesus has made between the Father and his people.

20:20 *showed them his hands and side.* Luke says that all the disciples had some doubts about whether what they were seeing was real (Luke 24:36–43). In any case, it's interesting that Jesus does for these disciples what Thomas later demands for his proof.

20:22 *he breathed on them.* As God breathed life into Adam at the first creation (Gen. 2:7), so now Jesus breathes spiritual life into his people at this, the re-creation of the people of God (John 1:12–13). ***Receive the Holy Spirit.*** The other Gospels do not mention the coming of the Spirit to the disciples, but Acts 2 indicates Luke saw this promise being fulfilled on the day of Pentecost, seven weeks after Jesus' resurrection. It is significant to note that the Greek word for "breath" and "spirit" is the same word, *pneuma*.

20:23 *If you forgive ... if you do not forgive.* As in Jeremiah 1:9–10, the power is not conferred to the person to act on his or her own, but as a spokesperson for God. The disciples are to pronounce forgiveness upon those who receive the Gospel. Likewise, to those who refuse the Gospel, they are to pronounce the words of warning just as Jesus did (8:24).

20:24 *Thomas (called Didymus).* The Hebrew word for "Thomas" and the Greek word *Didymus* both mean "twin." ***was not with the disciples when Jesus came.*** Thomas is often vilified because of the doubt he expresses in this story (v. 25). However, it needs to be asked what it says about Thomas that he was not with the other disciples at this time. Perhaps this indicates that Thomas was also a little less fearful than the others. In another context, it is Thomas who, when Jesus talks about going to Jerusalem to die, bravely asserts, "Let us also go, that we may die with him" (11:16).

20:26 *Though the doors were locked.* This indicates that Jesus' resurrection body was not limited in the way a normal physical body might be limited. He was able to enter a locked room and simply appear. Nevertheless his body could be felt (v. 27), and he ate (Luke 24:41–43). ***Peace.*** This was a common Hebrew greeting (vv. 19, 21). The term reflects the salvation that Christ's redemptive work achieves—total well-being and inner rest of spirit, in fellowship with God.

20:28 *My Lord and my God!* Thomas clearly affirms the deity of Jesus. This is the last of a series of confessions of faith that sum up what the author wants the reader to recognize about Jesus.

20:29 *blessed are those who have not seen and yet have believed.* The author applies the words to Thomas to the situation of his readers. They are not deprived because of never having seen Jesus. Indeed, he is with them through the Spirit (14:15–20), just as he was with the apostles.

Session 13
Jesus Reinstates Peter

Scripture John 21:1–19

LAST WEEK

In last week's session we discussed the story of Thomas and his doubt concerning the Resurrection. Only after he was able to touch Jesus' wounds did he declare, "My Lord and my God!" Jesus then reminded him, and future believers, that "blessed are those who have not seen and yet have believed." This week, in our final session, we will consider Jesus' reinstatement of Peter and the encouraging message this story has for us when we need a second chance.

ICE-BREAKER   15 Min.
Connect With Your Group

LEADER
Begin this final session with a word of prayer and thanksgiving for this time together. Choose one or two Ice-Breaker questions to discuss.

Jesus shared a special meal and precious time with the disciples in today's story. Take turns sharing more of your experiences in life as you begin this last session together.

1. What is the best memory you have related to fishing? What made the experience special to you?

2. If you could rate your fishing proficiency from 1 ("I catch 'em in the frozen food section) to 10 ("I could have landed Moby Dick"), how would you rate yourself?

3. What is your favorite food to eat around a campfire?

89

BIBLE STUDY   30 Min.
READ SCRIPTURE AND DISCUSS

LEADER
Ask a member of the group, selected ahead of time, to read aloud the Scripture passage. Then discuss the Questions for Interaction, dividing into subgroups of four or five.

While Jesus' resurrection was a joyous event for the disciples, it no doubt created some personal distress for Peter. He knew that Jesus was aware of his failure to stand by him when he was faced with death. But in the following story Jesus helps Peter to see the depth of his forgiveness, and that Jesus is one who gives second chances. Peter's second chance came in the form of being called to the service of Christ and his "sheep." Jesus was showing him that he still loved and trusted him. Read John 21:1–19 and note how Peter reacts to Jesus' mercy and forgiveness.

Jesus Reinstates Peter

21 *Afterward Jesus appeared again to his disciples, by the Sea of Tiberias. It happened this way: ²Simon Peter, Thomas (called Didymus), Nathanael from Cana in Galilee, the sons of Zebedee, and two other disciples were together. ³"I'm going out to fish," Simon Peter told them, and they said, "We'll go with you." So they went out and got into the boat, but that night they caught nothing.*

⁴Early in the morning, Jesus stood on the shore, but the disciples did not realize that it was Jesus.

⁵He called out to them, "Friends, haven't you any fish?"

"No," they answered.

⁶He said, "Throw your net on the right side of the boat and you will find some." When they did, they were unable to haul the net in because of the large number of fish.

⁷Then the disciple whom Jesus loved said to Peter, "It is the Lord!" As soon as Simon Peter heard him say, "It is the Lord," he wrapped his outer garment around him (for he had taken it off) and jumped into the water. ⁸The other disciples followed in the boat, towing the net full of fish, for they were not far from shore, about a hundred yards. ⁹When they landed, they saw a fire of burning coals there with fish on it, and some bread.

¹⁰Jesus said to them, "Bring some of the fish you have just caught."

¹¹Simon Peter climbed aboard and dragged the net ashore. It was full of large fish, 153, but even with so many the net was not torn. ¹²Jesus said to them, "Come and have breakfast." None of the disciples dared ask him, "Who are you?" They knew it was the Lord. ¹³Jesus came, took the bread and gave it to them, and did the same with the fish. ¹⁴This was now the third time Jesus appeared to his disciples after he was raised from the dead.

> ¹⁵*When they had finished eating, Jesus said to Simon Peter, "Simon son of John, do you truly love me more than these?"*
>
> *"Yes, Lord," he said, "you know that I love you."*
>
> *Jesus said, "Feed my lambs."*
>
> ¹⁶*Again Jesus said, "Simon son of John, do you truly love me?" He answered, "Yes, Lord, you know that I love you."*
>
> *Jesus said, "Take care of my sheep."*
>
> ¹⁷*The third time he said to him, "Simon son of John, do you love me?"*
>
> *Peter was hurt because Jesus asked him the third time, "Do you love me?" He said, "Lord, you know all things; you know that I love you."*
>
> *Jesus said, "Feed my sheep.* ¹⁸*I tell you the truth, when you were younger you dressed yourself and went where you wanted; but when you are old you will stretch out your hands, and someone else will dress you and lead you where you do not want to go."* ¹⁹*Jesus said this to indicate the kind of death by which Peter would glorify God. Then he said to him, "Follow me!"*
>
> John 21:1–19

LEADER

Refer to the Summary and Study Notes at the end of this session as needed. If 30 minutes is not enough time to answer all of the questions in this section, conclude the Bible Study by answering questions #6 and #7.

QUESTIONS FOR INTERACTION

1. What about this story is most surprising to you?
   - ❏ That the disciples were out fishing after Jesus had already appeared to them (20:19–29).
   - ❏ That the disciples did not recognize Jesus (21:4).
   - ❏ That Jesus could show professional fishermen where to catch fish (21:6).
   - ❏ That Jesus would reinstate Peter after what he did.
   - ❏ Other_____.

2. Why do you think Peter decided he wanted to go fishing?
   - ❏ To return to what was familiar.
   - ❏ To have some time to think.
   - ❏ He was hungry.
   - ❏ Other_____.

3. How do you think the disciples felt when Jesus told them to throw their net on the right side of the boat? What does it say that they did what he said?

4. Why does Jesus ask Peter three times if he loves him? What do you think Peter was feeling by the third time?

5. What does Jesus mean by the phrase "feed my sheep/lambs"? Why is it significant that Jesus is giving this task to Peter?

6. If you knew someone who could tell you how you were going to die, would you want to know? What would you do to prepare for that moment?

7. If Jesus said to you today, "Feed my sheep" what specifically would that mean for you? Where would you start?

GOING DEEPER: *If your group has time and/or wants a challenge, go on to this question.*

8. How do you know when to give someone a second (or third!) chance, such as Peter received; and when wisdom would say to find someone else to entrust?

CARING TIME   15 Min.
APPLY THE LESSON AND PRAY FOR ONE ANOTHER

LEADER

Conclude this final Caring Time by praying for each group member and asking for God's blessing in any plans to start a new group and/or continue to study together.

Gather around each other now in this final time of sharing and prayer and encourage one another to have faith as you go back out into the world, remembering that Jesus will be with you every step of the way and understands what you're going through.

1. What have you especially appreciated about this group?

2. Where is Christ calling you right now to "throw your nets" to live a more productive life for him? What help do you need to find this direction?

3. Where do you need a second chance in your life? How can this group assist you in prayer?

NOTES ON JOHN 21:1–19

Summary: It's one thing to tell someone that you forgive him or her. That is simply a matter of saying words, and can be relatively easy. It's another thing to show someone your forgiveness by giving that person a second chance. That's what Jesus did for Peter. As Jesus had predicted, Peter denied three times that he knew Jesus, while Jesus was on his way to his death. Luke says that after Peter did so, Jesus turned and looked straight at him (Luke 22:61). He was aware of Peter's perfidy and no doubt felt the pain of it as part of the suffering he went through on the way to the cross. Peter's failure was probably excruciatingly painful to him. We are told in Luke 22:62 that after it happened, Peter went out and "wept bitterly."

It is possible that the reason Peter decided to go out fishing in today's story was to try to forget and put it all behind him. But it was an act of mercy that Jesus didn't let Peter just forget, because he helped Peter to find real healing from his failure. Then by commissioning him to ministry, Jesus showed Peter that he still trusted him and valued the contribution that he could make. That is true forgiveness. That is also the forgiveness that Jesus offers us—a chance not only to put our mistakes behind us, but also to find full restitution by contributing to his kingdom.

21:1 Afterward. This is actually the same indefinite time reference John used to begin chapters 5, 6 and 7. When this appearance occurred is unclear. Since one of the themes in this section is Jesus' restoration of Peter, and since, like Mary in John 20:15, they did not recognize him at first, it may be that this event actually occurred before the climatic appearance to the disciples in John 20:19. **Sea of Tiberias.** Tiberias was a city founded on the shore of the Sea of Galilee in 20 A.D. by Herod. By the time this Gospel was written, this new name for the Sea of Galilee had become well known.

21:4 did not realize it was Jesus. Mary Magdalene had the same difficulty (20:14). Paul writes of the resurrection body being different than the physical body (1 Cor. 15:35–44), and this may explain why such difficulties happened.

21:6 Throw your net on the right side. Luke reports Jesus giving similar fishing advice to Peter and the others at the time he first called them (Luke 5:1–11.)

21:7 the disciple whom Jesus loved. This is thought to be John, the author of the Gospel. **It is the Lord!** As Jesus' voice opened Mary's eyes to recognize him (20:16), so here the enormous catch of fish revealed to the beloved disciple that the one with whom they were talking was the Lord.

21:11 153. Jerome reported that at the time it was thought that there were 153 species of fish. If this is meant as an allusion to this, it may have been intended to symbolize people from every race and culture, caught in the net of the kingdom and not lost ("the net was not torn").

21:12 breakfast. The Jesus that they met was no disembodied spirit. They could see him and hear him and eat with him. He had hands and feet that allowed him to kindle a fire on the beach. Jesus had been resurrected bodily. He had conquered death.

21:14 the third time. This is the third Resurrection account described in John's

Gospel (20:19–23,24–29). The post-Resurrection appearances are important for a number of reasons. For one thing, they are part of the proof of Jesus' resurrection (along with the fact of the empty tomb, the collapsed and empty grave clothes, etc.) Second, they show that Jesus had conquered death. He was not simply a disembodied spirit who appeared as a ghost-like figure, a hallucination or a vision. Third, they describe how it was that the disciples learned of their mission. Fourth, it was the encounter with the living Jesus that changed the disciples from frightened men in hiding to bold witnesses who changed the world. Finally, the post-Resurrection appearances show to all of us that Jesus is still alive and we can enter into a personal relationship with him even today.

21:15 *do you truly love me more than these?* This question is ambiguous, but Jesus is probably asking Peter if indeed he loves him more than the others do as Peter indicated in John 13:37. In asking this question, Jesus allows Peter the opportunity three times to pledge his love for him. It is significant that he is voicing his love for every one of the three times that he had denied him. ***Feed my lambs.*** After each query about his love, Jesus calls Peter to demonstrate that love by being a "good shepherd" to Jesus' sheep (followers.)

21:18 *you will stretch out your hands, and someone else will ... lead you where you do not want to go.* From the way early Christians dealt with passages like Isaiah 65:2 and Exodus 17:12, it is known that the stretching out of a person's hands was an early Christian idiom for crucifixion. This explains the author's comment on this quote in verse 19.

21:19 *the kind of death by which Peter would glorify God.* Peter would indeed lay down his life for Jesus at some point in time. Since it is believed that Peter was killed during Nero's persecution of Christians in the early 60s, this Gospel's first readers would have known the manner and reality of his death. ***Follow me!*** The important thing for the disciple, be it Peter or the reader of the Gospel, is to keep on following Jesus regardless of where the path might lead (12:26).

Personal Notes

Personal Notes